LIFE LESSONS OF A
LONE TROOPER

THE LEGACY AND FRUIT
OF YOUR LABOR

Elaine J. Clinger Sturtz

Janet -
Be strong + brave !
Elaine J. Sturtz

LIFE LESSONS OF A
LONE TROOPER

THE LEGACY AND FRUIT
OF YOUR LABOR

Elaine J. Clinger Sturtz

DECLARATION
PRESS

DECLARATION PRESS

Life Lessons of a Lone Trooper:
The Legacy and Fruit of Your Labor

Cover Design by Steven Fisher, MFA

ISBN-13: 978-0-9983102-5-1

In Memory
of
David D. Sturtz

My Husband and Best Friend

He made a difference in my life and in the lives of others.
This world is a better place because Dave lived, served and loved.

This book is dedicated to all the people he touched throughout his
life and those he touches in the fruit of his labor and his legacy.

Thank you, God, for the gift of a life well lived!

CONTENTS

ACKNOWLEDGEMENTS

Thank you, God, for the gift of David D. Sturtz. Thank you, God, for allowing our paths to come together and walk the journey of life. Amen.

Thank you to all the family and friends who shared stories, memories and the difference Dave made in their lives. Thank you for your willingness to allow me to share your words.

Thank you to my editors/proofreaders—Becki Fogle, my friend who is always willing to help me with my latest project, and Merilyn Clinger, my dear aunt who writes her comments along with the editing.

Thank you to Tom Rice, Rob Hartsell and Butch Collins for your assistance with Highway Patrol stories and memories.

Several of the photos in the book are from the Ohio State Highway Patrol. Thank you for permission to share these photos.

The cover design and artwork have been created by Steve Fisher. I discovered his artistic talent when he was a youth, and I was his youth minister in Marysville. It has been so enjoyable working with Steve in all of these creations. Thank you, Steve.

Thank you to my great-niece, Trista, for her artistic drawing of Dave on the lawnmower. God has blessed you with a wonderful talent.

Thank you to Great-Granddaughters, Brooklyn, Makenna, and Addisyn, for your beautiful drawings that are included in this book.

INTRODUCTION

I have two treasured material possessions from my Grandma Ruth Clinger—her rocking chair and her teapot. I had her desk until recently when I gave it to my niece who now has a material reminder of her Great-Grandma. These possessions have had an honored place in every home in which I lived. I even had a Grandma meditation room in one of our homes. Another treasured possession is my Dad's milk stool—one he sat on for years to milk cows. I also have two milk cans that bring back so many memories of my childhood on the farm. I have an afghan that I touch daily that my Mom crocheted especially for me.

Each possession, while very special and priceless to me, is just a material possession. They have little monetary value. What makes them priceless is who they represent and the difference the lives of my parents and my grandmother made in my life. The truly priceless physical reminder of my Grandma is her handwritten letters. She wrote letters to me while I was in college, seminary and through my first pastorate. They contained words of wisdom which I shared in my first book, *Love Lighted Path*. I have letters from my mom during this time which share everyday life and one letter from my dad.

Through the written words of my Grandma Clinger and my parents, I have tangible reminders of their lives and their view of life. The treasure is not in the material gifts, but in how they live on in my life through what they taught me and how they lived their lives. Their words took root in my life and now bear fruit. The fruit of their labor is evident in my life. They instilled in me a deep faith, a love for family, a strong work ethic, and a love for the land and the soil. Their lives have meaning and purpose, yes, in how they lived, but more in how they continue to live on in the lives they touched. They are my foundation.

My husband, David D. Sturtz, was a man of words, both spoken and written. Our relationship began through the written word. He wrote thousands of letters throughout his life. He wrote reports, completed investigations, wrote traffic tickets, interviewed thousands of people, wrote speeches and statements, made an abundance of phone calls, took notes, taught classes, and the list could go on and on. Dave's words had their foundation in his beliefs, values, morals, ethics and the influence of his parents and family.

His words live on through this book. This book is about a life well lived and the fruit of his labor that lives on in those my husband, David D. Sturtz, touched on his journey through this life. When we complete this earthly life, it is not the end of our influence. We continue to learn from those who have gone before us and use their knowledge and influence. We make decisions based on what we learned from them. We respond to others and to situations because of how we watched them respond. We continue to learn from them as we remember their lives and how they reacted, how they made something or how they relied on God in the struggles of life.

The full meaning of a person's life is revealed long after they are gone from our sight. They live on in our hearts as their spirit and love is within us to guide us. This is their legacy that continues through us. What we think, feel, believe, and dream are not just our own views, but they are a combination of the views of those who came before us and touched our lives. They are still bearing fruit in our lives.

Jesus tells us in John 15:16 (NCV), "I chose you. And I gave you this work: to go and produce fruit, fruit that will last...." The fruit of Dave's labor is evident in the stories told throughout the relationships of his life. All of life comes down to relationships, our relationship with God and our relationship with one another. God created us to live in relationship with one another.

Dave was a people person who talked with everyone and treated people with respect no matter their status in life. He was quick to get to know a person and find out about his or her life. People were drawn to him through his personality, his smile, his laughter and his stories. He could tell a story and make you feel you were there with him. Dave was a storyteller with detailed explanations and recall. He would pull you into the story. He had a story for every occasion and event.

This book is filled with stories Dave himself told, stories from family and friends and stories from those who worked with Dave and with whom he had a relationship. Some of the stories are my memory of Dave telling the story. The stories written may be different than you remember them, and that is okay. Dave told them differently to make a different point or life lesson. This book is not a biography, but an example of how one life made a difference in this world. Our lives are to be lived in relationship with one another and make a difference. We are put on this earth with the purpose of making a difference in the lives around us. There needs to be evidence of fruit from how we lived.

The first chapter explains the essence of Dave which will be explained in detail throughout the book. Dave was not perfect, but the life lessons from God are perfect foundation stones for our lives. Dave had a respect for himself, a respect for others, and a deep respect and love for God.

I hope you laugh and cry as you read this book and the stories. I hope you remember a story and how Dave told it and smile. I hope you remember a story from your own life and of other people who made a difference in your life.

The hope for this book is that these stories will challenge you to see the fruit of the lives that came before you and to produce fruit from your life that will last in future generations.

CHAPTER 1

THE ESSENCE OF THE MAN

David D. Sturtz

David Sturtz was known by many names and titles throughout his life. His first was son. He was the third son of Walter and Helene Sturtz and was born in Roscoe Village outside of Coshocton, Ohio. His second name was brother. He was the brother of Donald, James and Kenneth. He was a student and an athlete, playing football, basketball, and baseball. He was known as "Sturtzee" to his high school best friends, Herb Chilcote and Gary Cosmar. He became a college student and football player at the University of Cincinnati and was called "The Preacher" because he didn't do any of the wild things other players did and he stood up for others, living out his principles and values.

He received the title of Patrolman in 1959 when he graduated from the State Highway Patrol Academy. He rose through the ranks of Patrolman, Academy PT instructor, Corporal, Sergeant, Lieutenant, Captain, and became The Major on April 7, 1975. DD Sturtz retired on January 16, 1988. He gained the respect of troopers and was a leader not just in name but in how he lived and treated others. He became a legend in his own time.

David had the title of husband when he married Iris Craig in 1958, and then father with the births of his daughter, Gretchen, and son, Craig. He later enjoyed the title Grandpa with the birth of O'Shay and Christopher. After Iris died in 1989, Dave married Elaine Clinger. He gained the title of Pop with the birth of three great granddaughters: Brooklyn, Makenna and Addisyn.

David accepted the title as the First Inspector General when he was appointed on August 8, 1988 by Governor Celeste. He accepted the challenge to build something out of just a piece of paper. He continued in his work career with the titles of Assistant Safety Director for the City of Columbus and Training Coordinator for TSA (Transportation Security Administration).

The title of storyteller and the giver of life lessons were titles Dave loved. His choice of phrases and the way he told a story made you feel you were truly in relationship with him and wanted to know more and use what he was sharing for good. The title of friend was most cherished by Dave.

David D. Sturtz made a difference in this world. He stood for honor, truth and integrity. He challenged you to grow and learn and want to do your very best.

Dave was a child of God. He gave his heart and life to Jesus as His Lord and Savior. He continued to grow in his faith throughout his life. He found his purpose in life was to be in relationship with others and to strive to be an influence and a support to others on their journey. Dave completed his earthly journey, but his legacy lives on in all he influenced. We are better people because David D. Sturtz was in our lives.

"I command you to be strong and brave.
Don't be afraid, because the Lord your God
will be with you everywhere you go."
(Joshua 1:9, NCV)

A Man of Words

*"Let the words of my mouth and the meditation of my heart
be acceptable in thy sight,
O Lord, my rock and my redeemer."
(Psalm 19:14, RSV)*

Dave was a man of words. He always noted time and date of phone calls and wrote down words from the conversation. He kept a phone log and a calendar.

We met through words. I gave a talk on the Walk to Emmaus Spiritual Weekend in which Dave participated as a pilgrim. I sent cards to Dave sharing that I was praying for him and his wife, Iris, through her battle with cancer. Then a sympathy note at her death. I sent a letter to Dave when he was a team member on the Emmaus Walk, and that began our relationship. We talked for hours on the phone before we ever dated in person. We sent letters for months as we dated, and I still have all those letters. Words of growing love and commitment were written on those pages. Dave was straightforward and knew that this relationship was what he wanted. He was not afraid to share his feelings.

Throughout our marriage, Dave wrote notes of encouragement, forgiveness, and thankfulness. Instead of gifts for birthdays, anniversaries, Christmas and special holidays, we wrote a letter and expressed our love and commitment to one another.

I carry in my Bible the last card Dave wrote to me on our Twenty-Fifth Wedding Anniversary. It said in part,

"My Dearest Elaine,

Thank you for the great gift of twenty-five years of your love and care. You mean the world to me....
Love...."

—Dave

When Dave was in the hospital on February 14, 2015, he wrote me a note on a paper towel:

"Elaine,

Be My Valentine.

Thank you for your love, loyalty and trust. You are my Rock, my Life and Love.

Where God is taking us is our Destiny. Joshua 1:9 is my blessing given to me by you so many years ago. Thank you for being you. Love...."[1]

—Dave

Even in the midst of diagnosis, hospital, and infection, Dave found paper and pen to write words of love and thanksgiving.

Dave wrote hundreds of letters over his lifetime. He wrote letters of accommodation, thanking people for kindnesses, for speeches and for what they had done for him or others. Dave was never afraid to write what he thought whether good or bad. He was confident in his words. Dave wrote letters expressing the wrong that others had done. He said what he felt and never held back his words when truth needed to be spoken.

---

[1] This notation was also written on the note: "2/14/15 12:00 Noon, Mt. Carmel East – Room #516."

Writing also helps us take what is swirling around in our head and define it. It makes our thoughts real when we write them down and helps us to focus on what we want to express. I was a person of words before meeting Dave. I have written sermons, poems, books, and cards and letters throughout my ministry. Sending a card in the mail with a handwritten note is a personal gift of love given to another person. You let them know you took the time, effort and thought to write words of encouragement and hope to them.

God understands the importance of the personal gift of love. In the Gospel of John, we read these words, "And the Word became flesh and dwelt among us, full of grace and truth..." (John 1:14, RSV) God spoke the world into being through His Word and then shared His Word, Jesus, with the world in the flesh. Notice the words *"grace and truth"* in that verse. Grace is unconditional love and forgiveness which stands on the rock of truth. Dave's words were on this rock of truth.

Life Lesson

- From Dave, I have learned to write more letters and to write direct and honest feelings. I have learned to write letters that state the facts and are succinct. Letter writing is becoming a lost art. In honor of Dave, write more letters. They become part of your legacy.

Life Scripture

"I command you to be strong and brave.
Don't be afraid, because the Lord your God will be with you
everywhere you go."
(Joshua 1:9, NCV)

When Dave and I were first married, he packed his lunch in a brown bag each day. He preferred to eat at his desk at work so he could continue doing his paperwork. I began to write a scripture verse on a note card each day and put it in his lunch bag. Dave saved these cards but one card he kept in his wallet for twenty-five years. It was Joshua 1:9.

Dave said this verse described his life. He always knew God was with him and that he had been strong and brave because of God's presence.

This verse took on a new significance when Dave was diagnosed in February, 2015 with brain tumors. While in the hospital, I put this verse on blue cardstock paper and posted it in his room. He brought it home with him, and it was placed on the bathroom door. Each day Dave would read this verse aloud and remind himself to be strong and brave.

As Dave declined, I remember him standing by the bathroom door attempting to read the words with his vision blurred because of the tumors. But I knew as he tried to read, the verse was already in his heart and soul. Many days tears would stream down his cheeks as he read that verse, but he had the assurance that God was with him through it all.

That same blue cardstock paper with the verse is posted on my bathroom door today. I read that verse every day knowing God is with me. It is his strength that makes me strong and brave in this new chapter of life.

As I was reading from the book of Joshua, I discovered the hope in a verse just before this: "Just as I was with Moses, so I will be with you. I will not leave you or forget you." (Joshua 1:5, NCV) God was with Moses and now assured Joshua He was with him. God was with Dave, and God is with me as I travel this new chapter of life.

Life Lesson

- God writes His Word upon each of our hearts.

Testimony of Faith

On Sunday, July 9, 2000, Dave was asked by Pastor Judy Shook to share his testimony in the worship service at Reynoldsburg United Methodist Church. This is Dave's testimony:

> Good morning. My name is David Sturtz. I have been a member of this Church since 1973. I have had family members baptized, married and buried at this Church.
>
> I accepted Jesus as my Savior when I was nineteen years old. The greatest influence on my acceptance of Jesus in my life was from the actions and personal guidance of my older brother, Don. I have tried to live the life of a Christian as best I can, but I feel that I was tested several years ago to my outer limits.
>
> During a three-and-a-half-year period of time, my father died, my mother died, my very best friend died, my mother-in-law died, and finally my wife, Iris, died. Some were heart attacks, and some were cancer related. All were terrible losses to me personally. This Church surrounded me each time with prayers, cards and a tremendous amount of

love. Each time I carried on because of my faith in God. I knew my loved ones were no longer suffering here on earth and were now in heaven.

However, I was tested to my outer limits when several years ago, Elaine and I were on vacation in Florida. We received a telephone call from my son, Craig. He advised us that we needed to come home right away. His son, our grandson, Jonathan Craig, who was eleven months old, had swallowed a small toy and choked to death. This was a crushing blow to all of us.

Now, I had recovered and had accepted all of the previous deaths, but this time my questioning of the Lord was hostile and angry. I could not accept the death of this little boy that Elaine had just baptized only eight months before. He was a happy, loving little boy. Everyone who saw him loved him. Now he was gone from us all.

I was struggling with my faith until our grandson, Christopher, who was five years old at the time, opened my eyes with his clear and childlike love. At the funeral home, before the casket was closed the final time, he placed his favorite hat in the casket to keep his brother's head warm. He also placed a nickel in the casket so when his brother got to heaven, he could buy himself some milk.

Chris' love for his brother brought me back from a dark side where I was traveling. He made me realize the great love God has for each of us. His actions let me know that there is a Heaven, and that there is a loving God that gives us all "milk" and warmth when we need it. For me he used a five-year-old boy to teach me a lesson that I will always hold in my heart.

Through the childlike faith of his grandson, Dave experienced the presence of God in the midst of the pain and hurt. While Dave had accepted Jesus as his Lord and Savior many years before, he realized he was still growing in understanding of his faith. He was open to being taught by a five-year-old.

Dave continued to grow in his faith throughout our marriage as we placed Christ at the center of our lives and marriage. Dave had a personal relationship with Jesus, and a deep respect for God.

> *"Respect for the Lord will teach you wisdom.*
> *If you want to be honored, you must be humble."*
> *(Proverbs 15:33, NCV)*

Because of Dave's faith and respect for the Lord, he gained respect as a person. Dave lived his faith. He stumbled and made mistakes, but he asked for forgiveness and was given grace. Dave had a foundation to his life and was grounded in his faith. He believed he was a child of God and, therefore, respected himself and respected others.

Life Lesson

- Ground yourself in your faith in Jesus Christ. Be willing to learn and remain childlike in your faith. God will walk you through the hurts of life.

The Storyteller and Giver of Life Lessons

I remember dinners with retired Highway Patrol and their spouses in our home. The women would sit at one table and the men at another. This made it easier for the men to tell their stories. At the conclusion of the meal, if you were listening, you could hear one of the men say, "Remember the airplane and the ashes...."

The next thing you heard was laughter and someone slapping their leg. These retirees didn't need the whole story; they knew it just by a few words. But soon, there was silence, a clearing of the throat, and the booming voice of Dave would begin, "I was stationed at...." and Dave had everybody's attention as he described in detail an event of his Highway Patrol Career. Details included what everybody was wearing, what they ate at the meal, the day and time of the event, and concluded with how it made an impact on his career or the life of the person in the story.

Dave was a storyteller. He commanded the attention of everyone in the room when he spoke. He did not ask for everyone's attention, but when he spoke people listened. Dave had a presence about him and became known for his stories. People enjoyed hearing about his adventures on the highway patrol, his life stories, his investigations, and wanted his opinion on current events. Dave had an intense memory for details which made a great story. You felt like you were present in the story, and you would even jump when he talked about being hit with a door knob.

When Dave was about to tell a story, he leaned forward and straightened up in his chair. I have a picture of him leaning toward several people as he was sharing a story. He used his arms and legs in telling the story. He was all in when it came to what he was sharing. Leaning in is found in the Bible when John was reclining with

Jesus at the table and "leaned closer to Jesus" (John 13:25) to ask who Jesus was talking about. Leaning is with the intent to know and understand and share. Dave wanted the listeners to not only hear the story but understand what it meant in his life and how it could influence their lives.

Dave embellished some of the stories to make them more interesting, but most were amazing events in his life. Dave told stories for a purpose. He wanted to make a point and wanted to share knowledge and meaning with the hearers. The Bible is filled with stories of the lives of people and the stories of Jesus. The purpose is to learn about God and grow closer to Him. It is to learn from those who came before us.

Dave loved to tell bedtime stories to his two grandsons, O'Shay and Chris, when they were young and stayed overnight at our home. O'Shay describes these stories:

> Grandpa's stories were plots straight out of an
> Indiana Jones movie scene where Chris and I were
> the two main stars. He transformed Chris and me
> into comic book heroes who saved the day.

In the stories someone always was in need and someone was always the hero. During this time, Chris had a hamster named Ray. Dave would even make Ray the hero in many of the stories, which thrilled a little boy who loved his hamster.

Life Lesson

- Listen to the people around you who tell stories from their lives and learn from the stories.

Wisdom

"Wisdom begins with respect for the Lord,
and understanding begins with knowing the Holy One.
If you live wisely, you will live a long time;
wisdom will add years to your life.
The wise person is rewarded by wisdom,
but whoever makes fun of wisdom will suffer for it."
(Proverbs 9:10-12, NCV)

This Bible verse is highlighted in the Bible Dave carried to church and used on a regular basis. Wisdom and knowledge were at the essence of Dave. He valued knowledge and strived to learn and grow all his adult life.

As a high school student, he only worked hard enough to pass each class or test in order to be eligible to play sports. Later in life, Dave stated,

> I wish I would have studied more. Along with the studying, I wish I would have gotten better grades because I was more capable than I produced.

Dave knew it was within him, but at the time his focus was on sports and his athletic ability. As an adult, Dave grew in wisdom and understanding through the influence of his mom and her love for reading:

> My mom was an avid reader. She read everything and knew about countries she had never visited. She read everything in the library. They had to order books for her because she had already read all the books. Even when she was unable to read, she listened to books on tape.

Dave loved to read. That statement should read, "DAVE LOVED TO READ AND READ AND READ!" He read constantly and through the years acquired a library of over two thousand books. He loved history, the American Indians, investigations, biographies, and cowboy stories. He read about good winning over evil. He would read and find a reference to a book and search for that book. His favorite store was Half Price Bookstore. He would buy books, read them, and then sell them back and then buy more books.

He read for his careers. It was through his reading he learned the laws of the state, gained knowledge of investigations, and developed his leadership training. He read every major Ohio newspaper while Inspector General. Reading equaled knowledge and how he gained wisdom and understanding.

Life Lesson

- Read. Read. Read.

The Man

When Dave walked into a room, you knew it. He did not announce himself. It was just his presence that commanded attention and respect. When Dave would come home from an event, he would tell me his right arm hurt. He said he shook hands with so many people. He would say, "I just stepped into the door, and people started coming toward me." Even in his teenage years, everybody wanted to be around him. He had an outgoing personality, a great smile and loved life.

Dave always gave credit to his parents for instilling in him a strong foundation of life. He grew up in a loving and caring environment. He was blessed with a strong will and spirit. Dave recognized later in life the gifts God had blessed him with and how those gifts had sustained him throughout his life.

Dave's brother Don describes him:

> Dave's greatest gift was his attitude. He approached life with enthusiasm and an unquenchable drive to do his very best in whatever activity was at the moment. This included a deep-seated desire to do what was right in all circumstances—even when the decisions were difficult and hurtful to him personally.

I will be sharing throughout this book many different qualities and gifts possessed by Dave that are part of his legacy and were used to make a difference in this world and the lives he touched. When we recognize qualities in other people that we want to emulate, it is then that their lives make an impact and leave a mark.

Dave was a person of order and obedience. He followed the rules and taught the commands. One scripture that describes Dave's life is from Psalm 19:7-9 (NCV):

> The teachings of the Lord are perfect; they give new strength. The rules of the Lord can be trusted; they make plain people wise. The orders of the Lord are right; they make people happy. The commands of the Lord are pure; they light up the way. Respect for the Lord is good; it will last

forever. The judgments of the Lord are true; they are completely right.

Being in law enforcement for over forty-seven years of his life, he taught, followed the rules, orders and commands. He earned respect and made judgments.

One deeply rooted quality of Dave was his loyalty. Dave was devoted to his family, his friends, and his work. Dave was faithful to God and to the core of who he was. He always tried to do his best and to be his best. This was evident in how others were drawn to him. He became the "go-to" person who was trusted. When people did not know what to do or whom to call, they called Dave. Our phone would ring because someone needed guidance or advice. Dave would figure it out. Dave and I became the "go-to" people because of our commitment and compassion for people. Caring for people became and continues to be one of the callings in my own life.

Dave knew who he was and had confidence in his abilities and strengths. He had a strong foundation of faith, love and values. He was humble and did not need others to build him up. He loved people and enjoyed the companionship of so many lifelong friends and family. Dave was genuine, and people loved him for these qualities.

Life Lesson

- Be who you were created to be and enjoy your life.

Reflection

Rarely do we have the opportunity to know how others see us and what difference we have made in their lives. Dave had the gift of receiving hundreds of letters and cards from people in all chapters of his life when he was diagnosed with brain tumors. Many of these letters contained stories that I will be sharing in this book. I read to him how he had made a difference in the lives of others thus giving his life meaning and purpose. I have also received cards and notes from people since Dave's death describing the impact Dave made on their lives. In this chapter I share some of these descriptions to give you a flavor of the essence of Dave.

> "A word I would use to describe Dave is loyalty. He had many talents, but one talent was to understand people and see the core of a person. God made him a lover of people. He was supportive and would say, 'I'm here for you'."
>
> —Ray Belfrage

> "Dave was a man who demanded respect and earned it every moment of his life. He left a legacy of unwavering integrity, hard work and a life defined by his faith."
>
> —Caitlin Woods

> "Being around Dave made you a better person."
>
> —Jim Ricket

> "He taught me compassion, strength and love for all the 'black & grey'."
>
> —Gary Smith

"Dave was and is a man of character, a man who is mentally and physically strong, a man of intellect, a caring man, a strict man, and in fact, a man of God."

—John Magaw

Words Used to Describe Dave

Sweet, gentle, honorable, gentle giant, loving, kind, great man, truly cared about people, godly man, blessed to have known him, legend, my hero, made this a better world, honest, tough, faithful friend, truthful, outgoing, friendly, enthusiastic, open minded, dedicated, integrity, loyal, courageous, strong, mentor, and compassionate.

Life Lesson

- Live so that when you die, people can recognize the difference you made in their lives.

CHAPTER 2

FOUNDATION STONES OF LIFE

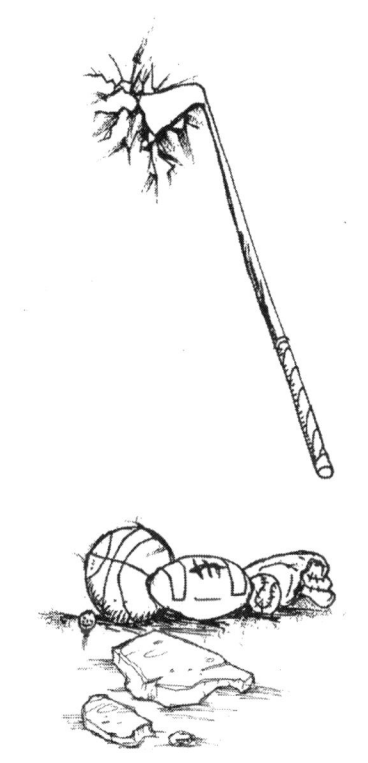

The Sturtz Family Legacy

- To be Obedient to God
- To love one another with unconditional love
- To support each other with strength and courage
- To always be fair and honest with our opinions
- To share individual joys and happiness with all
- To show others the Character and Honesty of the Sturtz Family
- To help others in Christian love and unselfishness
- To speak the truth and take responsibility for what we do
- To always honor the Sturtz Family Legacy

(Written by Dave for a Christmas Gift to
his children & grandsons)

Love of Parents

"Honor your father and your mother, that your days may be long in the land which the Lord your God gives you."
(Exodus 20:12, RSV)

Dave was the third son born to Walter and Helene Sturtz. He was born on the kitchen table in the family home in Roscoe Village, Ohio on May 6, 1937. This date in history is significant because the Hindenburg caught fire and crashed. This made worldwide news while in little Roscoe Village David Dale Sturtz was born. The Hindenburg was a moment in history, but the life of David D. Sturtz continues to make an impact long after his life has been completed on earth. Dave grew up in the 1940's and 1950's in the small town of Coshocton with his three brothers, Don, Jim and Ken. Dave loved his parents deeply. I will let Dave explain his parents in his own words:

> I had a Mom and Dad who loved me. I learned from my Mom and Dad strength of family love. My Dad loved his Mom and my Grandma Kubic (his mother-in-law). My Grandma Kubic was one of his greatest friends. And I loved my Dad because he showed such great love and respect for both of these women. The only two times I saw my Dad cry was at the funerals of my two grandmas.

Dave had a foundation of love, and he shared that love with his own family.

> My favorite memory of my Mom is her laughter. Her laugh was a happy laugh. It made you feel good, and it made you feel happy. Her laughter was the laugh of love. When I heard my Mom's laughter, I knew that all was well.

Dave inherited the laughter of his mom. Dave had an infectious laugh that made you laugh with him. It was always funny when he got tickled at something he said and was able to laugh at himself.

> My father was quiet but strong. The image I have of my father is that of a protector. He worked hard at every job he ever had and he was always an excellent provider for his family. He never complained. My Dad had several jobs that I can remember. First, he was a deep shaft coal miner. He was also a factory worker, a tavern owner and a security guard. Whatever job my Dad had, he worked hard and earned his money. I was always

proud of my Dad. My Dad's attitude was not to hurt or injure or make anyone feel bad. He had a slow sly smile that once you saw it, you trusted him. My Dad was a hard worker. He often said, "If someone pays you for a job, do the very best you can."

A foundation stone for Dave's life that came from his dad was that of a hard worker. Dave always gave everything to his work and excelled in all his careers.

I learned from my parents to be proud of who I was, and to never bring harm or shame to the Sturtz name. My greatest fear as a boy was failing to live up to what the Sturtz name meant. My fear was not living up to the expectations of my Mom and Dad and my brothers. Both of my parents often said, "You are a Sturtz so act like one. If you do good, we will all be recognized for your good. And if you do bad, it will be likewise."

The Sturtz name was a foundation stone for Dave. Be proud of who you are. Recognize that what you do has an effect on others in the family.

I was greatly influenced by my parents' words and actions. I was told that I was a Sturtz. Their attitude about our name led me to believe you do not lie, steal, or cheat. I wanted to be an honest and truthful person and uphold the Sturtz name. I would like to be remembered as a person who told the truth, stood by my principles and sometimes stubbornly, but people would know where I stood on issues and in difficult times. These feelings were taught to me by my parents, Walter and Helene Sturtz.

Through his parents, Dave built the foundation of truth, honesty and values. He learned to stand strong in the face of adversity.

Life Lesson

- The family unit is where the foundation stones of our lives are developed. Teach children the value of who they are and the strength in honesty and truth.

Childhood Memories

Dave loved growing up in Coshocton. He played with his brothers and the neighborhood kids. He played football, kick the can, baseball and basketball. He enjoyed riding his bike and swimming in the quarry. He never wanted to go home during the summer while he was playing to get lunch or something to drink.

> I would go up to any house, knock on the door and tell the lady who answered the door that I was a Sturtz boy and could I have something to drink. Living in a small town in the 1940's and 1950's, everyone knew everybody and it was a safe place. The lady would invite me inside and give me a glass of lemonade and some cookies. Sometimes I would tell them I was hungry, and I would be given a sandwich.

Dave learned in his childhood to be friendly and talk with everyone. He also learned to ask for what he needed and not be afraid of people.

> As a family we took long drives together. My Dad loved to drive. It was nothing for us to jump in the car early Saturday morning and before the day

was over we could be in Kentucky, West Virginia or even Virginia. There always seemed to be something to eat. Mom would pack a lunch, and we would stop to buy something to drink. It seemed like my Dad could drive forever and never get tired. He never liked to stop so we could go to the bathroom. In one of the cars, he drilled a hole in the floor so we boys could "pee" while we travelled. It was always fun to look out the back window and see how long the wet streak went from my brothers. We would laugh and talk and each got our turn to sit up front with Mom and Dad. We would entertain ourselves by the scenery. These trips were always great because by the time we got home, we were a closer family. Not only did we have family love, but we developed friendships.

Dave developed his love for driving from his dad. Like his dad, he also did not like to stop on trips.

When we lived at 215 S. Vine Street, my Mom and Dad bought the first television set in the neighborhood. It did not take long for the front room where the television set was to have as many as 18-20 people crowded in there to watch Milton Burle on the Texaco Hour. Grandma Kubic would pop popcorn in a large iron skillet. She would melt oleo over it, salt it, and everyone would eat it. When it was gone, she made more. For me, it was not so much the T.V. set or the program, but the great fun I had getting to know our neighbors and hearing their laughter. It taught me a great lesson from my Mom and Dad. It is great to share with others who do not have what you have.

Dave learned from his parents to share the joys of life with others and to focus not on the possessions but on the relationships.

Trouble and Truth

Dave remembered getting in trouble with his parents. They were angry and disappointed in him for doing something wrong and then lying about it.

> The trouble I got into was that I was throwing an old golf club into a tree trying to knock some apples to the ground. Instead of knocking the apples to the ground, I threw the golf club clear over the tree and through a big bay window of an elderly lady's house. I ran home scared, not knowing that the elderly lady was watching me throw the golf club into her tree. By the time I ran home, the lady had already called my mom. I was asked if I had just done anything wrong and I said, "No, I did not."
>
> And my mom said, "What about the golf club you threw through the window?"
>
> And I said, "It wasn't me, I wasn't near that house."
>
> My mom told me the lady had called her, and my heart sank. I confessed. My punishment was that I had to go back to the lady and apologize. In order to pay for the damage of the big window, I mowed her lawn the rest of the summer for free. The lady felt sorry for me and would bring me something to drink every time."

Through this childhood experience, Dave learned to be honest and tell the truth even if you know you will get in trouble. He learned never to lie to his parents.

> As a boy, I got into fist fights, rock throwing fights and B-B gun fights with the kids who lived in "Zerbyville" or "Zerby" addition. I participated in all of these fights and some of them I started. The Zerby kids didn't like us because they thought we were richer than they were. I was always on the alert for Milligan because he was meaner than a snake. My favorite hideaway was in the back of the factory called the American Art Works. My friends and I built a treehouse about twenty-five feet off the ground from scraps of metal and wood we found. It was the best tree house, but it became my biggest nightmare one day. I ran to the tree house one day and was the first of my friends there. Along came four Zerby addition kids. Three of them had B-B guns. They began shooting into the treehouse. The BB's would zing off the metal walls and hit my arms and legs, stinging me. The fourth kid was throwing rocks at the outside causing loud banging noises. After enduring this for half an hour which seemed like a half day, my friends arrived and ran off the enemy.

Dave learned to defend himself but also knew when he needed the help of his friends.

> One time in elementary school, I got in trouble at recess time. While playing football, my brand new and favorite shirt was ripped by a boy I did not like. I immediately started hitting him. The school ground supervisor tried to break up our fight. By accident, I kicked her in the shin. By that time,

other teachers had come out of the school building and broke up the fight. My punishment was that I had to clean all the blackboards of chalk writings and clean out all the erasers for the rest of the school year. For some reason, I enjoyed doing this punishment because how I cleaned the erasers was by smacking the two erasers together. I would come home with chalk dust all over me.

Dave learned to take the punishment for what he did wrong and turned this one into something enjoyable.

Responsibility

Dave recognized the work ethic in his dad early in his life. Dave had chores around the house, but his first paying job was being a tavern cleaner.

My first real job where I earned real money was helping my Dad on Sundays clean up the Sturtz Tavern after the crowd had left on a Saturday night. I swept the floor, cleaned off the tables, and washed the table tops. I washed all of the glasses and refilled all the pop containers. My Dad never let me work with the beer. I also cleaned the grease off the hamburger grill, took the change out of the juke box, counted it and marked it in a book. I was paid $2.00 for this work. Most of the time I would find from $5 to $8 of loose change in the booths and on the floor, and I was allowed to keep it all. My Dad called it my bonus. So, my first job was a tavern cleaner. I liked doing it because I was with my Dad.

Dave took responsibility early in life but he also saw a greater purpose to his work. It was not about the work, it was the time he spent with his dad in his first job that meant the most.

> When I was fourteen, there were about eight of us guys hired for the summer to work for the school and ball fields. Coach Warden was the boss. One day, we were all standing in a circle. Coach came down dangling keys and said, "Which one of you boys can drive this truck?"
>
> I raised my hand and said, "I can."
>
> He threw me the keys. I loaded up the sand and Stanley Thornsley and Gary Cosmar jumped in the truck with me. They reminded me that I didn't know how to drive. It was an old beat up Chevy pickup with the gear shift on the floor. I ground those gears all through town. It took me about three weeks not to grind the gears. I drove that truck every summer through my junior year. I delivered sand and school supplies all summer to the schools in Coshocton. I used the truck to rake the ball fields too. The gears finally fell out of the truck.

Dave was not afraid to take on a challenge or a responsibility. He did not know how to drive, but that did not stop him from taking on the job. He learned on the job and figured it out. This was a great foundation for him in his adult work life.

Brothers

Dave loved all three of his brothers. He used to say that his parents were so proud of the accomplishments of all four of their sons. Each brother was a professional going in his own direction.

When asked to describe his brothers in his growing years, Dave said,

> Don – I remember his friendship, his care and concern and his loving nature being the oldest brother.
>
> Jim – I remember him as an outstanding athlete who gave his best when the chips were really down. He always delivered when it was needed the most.
>
> Ken – he was the most innovative and resourceful. I think Ken is a combination of Don, Jim and I in his academics and athletic adventures. I love all three brothers in different ways, and I respect them all for their achievements.
>
> From Don I learned how to strive to be a Christian. He taught me to make God number one in my life. Through his example I accepted Christ as my Savior at age 19. As a grown man, my oldest brother, Don, is a Christian example to be followed. I never wanted to disappoint Don.

Dave saw the strengths in each brother and learned from them. Throughout his life, he stayed in contact with his brothers. All the brothers have respect for one another and are thankful for the foundation their parents gave them for life.

His oldest brother, Don, describes Dave:

> Dave grew in many ways—physically, morally and spiritually. You would always know where he stood on a given subject and he presented his viewpoint with conviction, sincerity and humility. He honored his Lord, his parents, and his family

by the life he lived and the goodness of his strong heart. He set an example for others to follow. His many friends, colleagues, and acquaintances could sense his integrity, decency and essential goodness.

His brother, Jim, described Dave:

Dave was a devoted family man, easy to know with a great sense of who he was. He was honest, kind and a dear brother to all. He was dearly loved, influenced so many and a great example for all of us.

His youngest brother, Ken shared about Dave:

Dave had an undeniable belief in right versus wrong, a sense of justice, and a bright line between the good and the bad. Our parents had instilled values in him that were deep rooted and inspired a lifetime of service to his family, his job, his church and his community. I enjoyed a relationship with Dave as his younger brother, a position in the family that provided for a unique insight into Dave's character. I was proud to call Dave "brother" and enjoyed being with him over the decades as life marched on. His accomplishments were many, in sports, in career, and most importantly to me, his family. He was without a doubt a big part of the "glue" that bound all of us together.

The bond that held these four brothers together came from the love and values instilled in them by their parents. In the last month of Dave's life, the four brothers spent a weekend together. They told stories and memories of childhood, their parents and the blessings of being a Sturtz. But most importantly, they shared their love and were able to say *"good-bye"* for now.

Sports

Dave's childhood and teenage years revolved around sports. His favorite sport was the one in season at the time.

> My activities were being an athlete. I cannot explain the joy I received participating in team sports. In basketball I was point guard. In baseball I was the catcher. In football, I was the quarterback and a defensive end. They gave me an outlet to display leadership, communication and to develop lifelong friendships with those I competed against. I enjoyed the challenge of high school athletics in representing my high school and my hometown of Coshocton. I was proud to be a Coshocton Redskin. My senior year, I was first string All-Central Ohio league in basketball and the second leading scorer in our league. In football, I was All-Central Ohio league defensive end. In baseball, I was an All-Central Ohio league catcher. I was Honorable Mention All-Ohio in all three sports. My senior year, my name was engraved on the Most Outstanding Athlete trophy for the high school. I was recruited by and offered a scholarship for football by the University of Cincinnati and played two years as a Bearcat.

Sports were Dave's focus in high school. He only studied when his eligibility was on the line to play sports. He would ace the test and be able to play in the game that week. Sports gave Dave the foundation of leadership, the desire to stay physically fit, and prepared him for his career in the Highway Patrol.

> I would come early for a football game. Coach Auble would wrap my ankles. One night he said, "Who do you want to be tonight?"
>
> I said, "I want to be Sturtz."
>
> "You are Sturtz," Coach said. "Who do you want to be on the field?"
>
> I said, "I want to be Max Speedy." (The half back for Cleveland). So, all through the game Coach called me Max Speedy.
>
> Then the next week, he would ask, "Who do you want to be tonight?"
>
> As a punko high schooler it gave me strength. Some nights I was Otto Graham or Donte Lavelli. I would put it in my mind that I was extra strong or fast. I was them and could run or pass like them.

Through his football coach, Dave found a way to build inner strength and confidence. He developed a way to focus and use the influence of others to guide and give him determination to win.

"Go out into the river where the Ark of the Lord your God is. Each of you bring back one rock, one for each tribe of Israel. They will be a sign among you."
(Joshua 4:5-6, NCV)

Life Lessons

- The love of family is the main foundation for our lives. The family unit teaches the values of truth, honesty, responsibility, sharing and working together. Through our interactions with others we learn right and wrong, to accept challenges and develop leadership.

CHAPTER 3

LOVE AND MARRIAGE

The Gift of Love

"Roses are red, Violets are blue
But neither one has anything on you."

Maybe not great poetry, but it came from the heart of Dave written on a scrap piece of paper for Valentine's Day.

"Roses are red, Violets are blue
Never, never in thousands of years
Could I stop loving you."

Another Valentine's Day poem written by Dave:

"Roses are very red, Violets are very blue,
There is no one else
For me but YOU!"

Dave liked the first two lines and used them often in his Valentine's poems!

Dave may not have been a great poet, but he knew how to express the love that was in his heart. Valentine's Day for us was not filled with roses, candy or gifts, but with a written expression of our love and devotion. The words of love have deeper meaning when the action of love is present.

Dave, in his words, had the ability to express how he received my love and how his life benefited from my love. I will let Dave express this in his own words written to me:

> You are my daily sunshine, you are the very air I breathe, you are the cool waters that quench my thirst. You fulfill every need, desire, or want that comes into my mind.

> You have been a shining bright light that has lit my path of life. Your smile gives me a feeling of warmth and love.
>
> God was very good to me when he placed you on my path of life. You make each step a joy, each mile a dream come true.
>
> You are my light on the hill. You give me direction and a reason to love.

Because of the love Dave and I shared and expressed to one another, our lives were enriched and strengthened. When one was struggling, the other was strong. We balanced each other and in this chapter of our lives, we needed each other.

In Ecclesiastes 4:7-9 (NCV), it states,

> Two people are better than one, because they get more done by working together. If one falls down, the other can help him up.... If two lie down together, they will be warm. An enemy might defeat one person, but two people together can defend themselves; a rope that is woven of three strings is hard to break.

God was at the center of our marriage and was the third cord that wove us together. We were united. We believed in one another and wanted the best for each other. We supported the endeavors of the other.

Now there were times Dave would *"get his nose out of joint"* as he called it and be jealous of the time I spent in ministry or caring for family. He would apologize and say he just wanted to be with me and for me to give my time to him. That is how Dave got involved in many ministries because he wanted to be with me. I have several letters of apology from Dave as he recognized his selfishness and supported my call to serve God and serve others in ministry.

The gift of love includes the admission of wrong, an apology, lots of grace, and sincere forgiveness. The admission is a confession of our humanness and how we allow our selfishness and self-centeredness to block our relationship and our love. A marriage centered on God puts the needs of the other above self which is sacrificial love.

I believe Dave and I had a sacrificial love within our marriage. We were not perfect and our selfish desires clouded our view at times, but we were striving toward this goal. We were hand-picked by God and were the best fit for each other to walk in this chapter of life together. Through Dave I gained confidence, strength and independence. Dave used to say, "I'm teaching you to be independent and do these things when I'm not here." (For example, paying bills, which he never liked doing.) We learned from each other and were not in competition with one another. We built the other up and rejoiced in the accomplishments of one another. We were each other's cheerleaders and encouragers.

Life Lesson

- Love the one with whom you choose to spend the rest of your life. Build each other up.

Relationship Surrender

In Coshocton High School 1955 Yearbook, these are the words beside David Sturtz' senior picture: "His Smile bewitches sweet ladies."

I saw his smile as he came toward me. I had just presented a clergy talk on The Walk to Emmaus spiritual weekend where he was a pilgrim. Before lunch, he walked toward me, with a big smile and said, "Hi! I'm Dave. I think you need a hug." And he hugged me and thanked me for sharing my story. I had shared in my talk about how a relationship had ended, and Dave felt I needed the reassurance that comes in a hug. And that is how I met Dave Sturtz.

I had met his wife, Iris, the month before when I was the Spiritual Director for The Women's Walk to Emmaus she attended. After these two weekends, I would occasionally see both of them at monthly Emmaus worship gatherings. I was invited to share a meal with them in their home along with another pastor. We had a connection because of our faith in Jesus.

When Iris was diagnosed with ovarian cancer, I sent cards of support and prayed for Iris and for Dave. Iris had seven operations, several rounds of chemo and radiation. She fought a courageous battle but was losing the war against cancer. When the reality of death became imminent, Iris began to prepare Dave for a future. Dave tells the story:

> I had to give Iris medication through her port every hour and flush it out during my twelve-hour shift of caring for her in our home. One night

Iris began the conversation about her dying. She said I was young and when she was gone that she wanted me to remarry. I didn't want to talk about it and walked out of her room. She said that I had to come back in an hour and she would continue the conversation. When I came back an hour later, Iris began again, "I want you to get married again. You have a lot to offer someone."

I didn't want to be having this conversation with her so I said flippantly, "So who do you think I should marry?"

Iris said, "I think Elaine Clinger. She is nice young lady."

"She's a minister," I shouted. "And she is so young."

And that began our journey. I had prayed in July of that same year, that if God wanted me to be single the rest of my life I would be all right with it. I had surrendered my relationship future to God. But God had other plans. Dave and I believe that God spoke through Iris, and we were chosen by God to be together.

Through cards and letters after the death of Iris, our connection began. On October 12-15, 1989, Dave was a team leader on the Walk to Emmaus and I wrote him a letter of support and encouragement. On his 1989 calendar, Dave wrote on October 14th, "Agape letter from Elaine J. Clinger." Then on October 16th, Dave wrote on his calendar, "5:45 pm telephone call to EJC – Celina." Later I would tell Dave that I was never home at that time but had to come home that day because someone spilled a drink on me. I came home to change to go to another meeting. I answered the phone, and to my surprise it was Dave.

His calendar on October 23rd: "Called Elaine J. Clinger *great response." And then on October 24th: "Called EJC – still very positive." Then on October 31st, Dave drove to Celina from his office in downtown Columbus for our first official date. We passed out Halloween candy and then spent the evening talking for hours.

Our relationship moved very quickly. We knew it was God who brought us together and planned for us to spend our lives in a love relationship. We were married on January 7, 1990 at St. Paul's United Methodist Church in Celina, Ohio.

Dave said to me later, "If you had been dating someone, I would have asked you to give me a chance."

The initial hug over three years before began our connection. It began a relationship even when a relationship was not yet possible. Iris planted the seed in Dave's mind while God had already planned the next chapter.

Life Lesson

- Surrender to God. Trust God with your relationships. God has a plan.

Connection

In a marriage, love is expressed in a variety of physical and tangible ways. The physical intimacy is a gift from God within the bond of marriage. The spiritual intimacy creates the foundation for the relationship. Dave and I placed God at the center of our marriage and our lives.

We struggled, sinned, forgave, gave grace, repented, grew, were blessed and through it all recognized God as our foundation and Jesus as our Lord and Savior. We read devotions together every day of our marriage, and we prayed together.

In the midst of our living, we learned that communication was central to our marriage, and it kept us growing. We talked every day. We shared about our day. We took time for each other. Some days we would sit on our deck and share devotions and talk. We enjoyed each other's company. On vacation we could sit for hours after dinner and just talk. Because God brought us together, there was always a deep spiritual connection – heart to heart.

Dave used to say to me, "Stick with me, kid," when life would get tough with his children or we were some place that was not where we wanted to be but needed to be. We were always connected. We stuck together throughout our marriage.

When Dave and I would walk anywhere together and something came between us or we took different routes around an object, Dave would say "bread and butter." I was to say something else that went together like "salt and pepper." I had never heard of this until Dave started doing it. The idea was that when something came between what went together—Dave and I—you had to say something to bring us back together. It was interesting all the different objects I found to say that went together. But what really went together were Dave and I. We were connected in a deep and abiding way through our love and spirits.

We were also connected by touch. In Psalm 139:5 (NCV), the Psalmist David writes, "You have put your hand on me." When Dave and I would go places together, there were many times in a crowd of people or at a gathering that he would place his hand on my lower back to gently lead me forward. He placed his hand on me as a sign of support and letting me know he was there for me. When Dave would introduce me to someone, he would touch my back as a way of presenting me to the person. It was his way of saying, "She is mine and I'm proud to introduce her to you."

Dave was a toucher. He did not like to hold hands though when we walked, because he said he wanted to be alert to what was around him. I know that was the law enforcement within him. We would always hold hands when we prayed. He would reach out and touch me when we were sitting at a long speech or sermon and just gently remind me that he was beside me. Touch connected us not just physically but emotionally and spiritually.

Life Lesson

- Stick with those God gives to you.

Loved by the Best

Since committing our lives to one another, there was never a day that Dave and I did not tell each other "I love you." Every day of our married life, we spoke these three words: "I love you." Life was not perfect because we were imperfect. There were moments we did not like each other or like what the other said or did, but deep within our hearts, we truly loved one another.

When I would say to Dave, "I love you," he would respond many times, "I love you more." Maybe he did. Since his death, I have come to realize the depth of our love and friendship. In life I loved him and who he was and how we interacted with one another. Now in his death, I love him more because I see what I truly had and how I grew and learned from our relationship. Dave can do nothing for me now, but his love remains in my heart and life.

One of Dave's favorite songs was recorded by country singer, Don Williams—"I've Been Loved by the Best." That is how we saw our relationship. We were loved by the best person for us at this time in our lives. We were best friends and enjoyed being together.

Many people talk about having a soul mate, that one special person for your life. I don't know if there is just one or maybe one for that chapter or time in your life. All I know is, God brought Dave and me together at the right time to help each of us on our journey and to experience the deep intimacy of love.

When Dave was nearing the end of his life, we began talking about life and death. He said he did not worry about me because I was strong, confident, independent, and had the faith to make it through. He started to talk about what my next chapter of life would be like and about someone else and I said to him, "I've already been loved by the best."

He said, "Thank you."

And we never returned to that conversation. Dave was the best for me. I learned to love and to know what it feels and means to be loved.

Life Lesson

- Say "I love you" to the people in your life. Express your feelings of love.

Wedding Anniversary

Each year on our wedding anniversary, January 7th, Dave and I would light our unity candle from our wedding and pray together. We would thank God for bringing us together and ask for God's blessings on another year of our marriage. Many years, we would share a meal of spaghetti in our home. This was the first meal Dave prepared for me when we were dating. Spaghetti was one of his favorites.

The unity candle reminded us that God was at the center of our lives and our marriage. The candle was given to us at a bridal shower by Sally and Bill Myers. They were like my adopted parents in college. Their love and marriage was an example for me and, therefore, how appropriate that the candle came from two people I loved so deeply. When Dave and I would light the candle, we renewed our vows through the light of Christ and renewed our commitment to one another.

On our wedding day, we wrote these vows and spoke them to one another:

> I commit my life totally unto you, here in the presence of God. I will always love you, need you and want to share my life with you. Together we will walk through this life as husband and wife, with God at the center of our marriage. I give to you now my faith, my life and my love.

On our anniversary, we recommitted to these vows that were the foundation of our marriage and life together.

Instead of giving anniversary gifts, we wrote a letter or card to one another. I have all of those in a memory box along with birthday and Valentine's cards. Dave was able to express his love. I share with you some of the words Dave wrote to me so that you will understand the depth of love that was in the heart of Dave. He loved and he was loved.

Here are a few excerpts from anniversary letters over the years written by Dave to me:

> "Look how far we have come as husband and wife. You are so dear to me. Neither my heart nor my mind can explain the deep, deep love that I hold for you. You fulfill my every desire and wish. I don't know how I could go on without you at my side."

> "I love your laughter. I love talking with you. I love being with you. I love how you are in your heart. I will never stop loving you, caring for you and needing you."

> "You are what God has granted to me and I am so thankful for his goodness. You are such a part of my total being. I can't imagine what a day or even an hour without you would be like. A dozen years have gone by, sometimes it seems we have been together forever, then other times it seems we have just started our journey together."

> "You are a strong person in many ways, caring, unselfish, giving, happy and in turn, all of your virtues make me a stronger and better person. I

love you so much and so deeply words cannot express how much. You are my sunshine, my air, my heartbeat."

"You have brought great joy and happiness to my heart each day of our married life. I love to hear you laugh, especially if I'm the one who made you laugh."

"You are my inspiration. I'm thankful to our God that He made our two paths into one. Our journey has been filled with some sorrow, grief, and minor obstacles; however, most of the journey has been filled with love and great expectations."

"I loved you when we first met, I love you right now, and I will love you forever."

"I cannot express to you in mere words the love and respect that I hold for you. You are dearer to me than the air I breathe each day. I love you so deeply that sometimes when I'm watching you and you don't know it, my heart actually aches and it becomes hard to breath."

"If I had a choice of anything in the world or you, I would always choose you."

"You never cease to amaze me. My love for you grows with each day, week, month and now years. God has blessed me by bringing you into my life and that we share love and a strong friendship."

"You keep me level in good times and not so good times. I love you, respect you and I'm grateful to God that he brought our two paths together and made one. Traveling life's highway with you is one trip that makes me happy."

"I know that God has placed us together. I pledge my continuous love and support until my last breath."

The words Dave wrote and that I wrote to him shared how we recognized the growth in one another through our love. We were grateful that God brought us together and we gave God the glory for blessing us with one another. Life was filled with struggles and joys that mingled together and formed the forever bond of love.

I Corinthians 13:8 (RSV) states, "Love never ends." The love Dave and I have for each other will never die. It will remain in my heart and strengthen me in the next chapters of my life.

Life Lesson

• Express your love. Write it down. Share it. Let those you love know what they mean to you. When you are gone, they will have letters that will sustain them in your love.

Safe Place

"Lord, you are my strength and my protection,
my safe place in times of trouble."
(Jeremiah 16:19, NCV)

The hugs of Dave were my safe place throughout our marriage. Dave gave the best hugs. When you were enveloped into his arms and received his bear hug, all became right with the world. He would say, "I'm here." His words gave me the assurance that no matter what was happening, we were in this together. I was never alone.

In the Bible, God gives the assurance that we are never alone and that He will protect us: "Let me hide under the shadow of your wings until the trouble has passed." (Psalm 57:1, NCV)

The safe place with Dave was more than a physical hug. He was the safe person to share what was happening in my work and in my thoughts. We shared and talked through what was happening around us and within us. As we talked, we knew the other was listening and would either give guidance or be willing to listen with a heart that cared.

The safe place was also being with one another. It was so comfortable being together and going to events and places together. As we drove into the driveway coming home from a trip or adventure, Dave would always say, "Thanks for taking me." It was not that he always enjoyed going, it was that he enjoyed being together. We never took each other for granted but found comfort in knowing that the other would be there and would be supportive.

The safe place was also a place of support and encouragement. Whenever I was about to lead a group, give a talk or sermon, or go to work, Dave would always say, "Do good." These were words of encouragement and words that expressed his belief in me and what I was doing.

It is a great gift to have a person in your life that is your safe place. A person, who believes in you, trusts you, encourages you and challenges you to grow and become who God created you to be. Dave was my place of safety.

Life Lesson

- It is important to have a safe place in your life. Be someone's safe place.

CHAPTER 4

THE MAJOR AND THE LEGEND IN THE OHIO STATE HIGHWAY PATROL

Life Plan

*"People may make plans in their minds,
but the Lord decides what they will do."
(Proverbs 16:9, NCV)*

Dave graduated from high school and had completed his second year of college at the University of Cincinnati. He planned to teach biology and coach high school football after he graduated. God had another plan.

I didn't choose the Highway Patrol, they chose me. I was on a football scholarship at the University of Cincinnati. I got into difficulty with two classes and had to decide if I go back to summer school to keep my eligibility. I came home and got a call to play in a fast pitch softball tournament and, being an athlete, I naturally played. I hit a long single and tried to make it into a double. I slid into second base and broke the second baseman's ankle. He was a Patrolman playing that position.

After the game was over, I went to the Coshocton Memorial Hospital to check on him. While I was there he recruited me. He said, "We are starting a brand-new program called Cadet Dispatcher and then you go into the ranks."

"No," I said. "I want to be a biology teacher and coach football. Thanks, but no thanks."

The Patrolman said, "You are a strapping young man. We need people like you."

"No. Sorry I broke your ankle, but no." I said.

That was a Friday night, and Saturday morning a first Sergeant showed up at our door. My dad said, "David, there is an officer out here."

"I didn't do anything, Dad."

He brought me an application. It was all filled out. All I needed to do was sign it. He said, "On Monday in Cambridge they are going to test people and we want you to come."

I said, "I'll take it, but I don't think I will be there."

The Sergeant said, "Son, you will be there." I signed the paper.

I showed up along with forty-seven other guys. When it was all done and over with, two of us passed the mental part, and I was the only one who passed the physical. I was one of the first cadet dispatchers hired. That was a Monday and the next Monday I reported to New Philadelphia. I stayed there a year and a half, and then went to the academy at Hartman Farms.

David began his career in the Ohio State Highway Patrol as a cadet dispatcher. Dave was the first Cadet hired under the new Cadet Dispatcher program. He graduated from the Academy on June 26, 1959. He began as a Patrolman, was the Academy PT instructor, and continued through the ranks of Corporal, Sergeant, Lieutenant, Captain, and became a Major on April 7, 1975. DD Sturtz retired on January 16, 1988.

Dave summarized his highway patrol career:

I had a wonderful career. I had a career nobody else has had in the Highway Patrol. Just because of the circumstances and the phone calls and the need, and I responded.

Life Lesson

- We can make plans but need to be open to new opportunities we never expected. God opens doors. We just need to be smart enough to walk through the door of opportunity.

Mentor

"You not only have to be right, you have to look right."
(Colonel R.M. Chiaramonte, Unit 364)

This was Colonel Robert Chiaramonte's statement that remained with Dave and many on the Highway Patrol. It was a statement of honesty and integrity. Dave followed this belief and looked up to his leader throughout his career. Disappointment came into the relationship, but this did not change what he had learned from his mentor and the respect he had for him.

Dave admired and respected Bob Chiaramonte from the beginning of his encounter with him. He was one of Dave's instructors at the Academy in 1959. This is what Dave shared about what then Lt. Chiaramonte said as an instructor:

> He talked of ethics and how people look at you. He talked about being honest and ethical. We were to treat an elderly man as you would treat a father and if you stopped a young lady, treat her as a sister.

At the dedication of the Lebanon Ohio State Highway Patrol new post in 1967, Colonel Chiaramonte said these words about D.D. Sturtz:

He is the youngest sergeant in the state (age 30), and one of the best. He has taken on every assignment with enthusiasm and has performed his duties with competence.

In a letter dated February 19, 1988, Colonel Bob Chiaramonte wrote to Dave:

"Dear David,

I recently heard about your retirement. It hit me with mixed emotions. You have given the State and the Patrol 29 outstanding years. Your qualities attracted my attention early on and continued through the years. You are what most young men would like to be and most old men wish they had been. I have known about 3000 men in the Patrol and you rate among the very best in my opinion. I am proud of you and will always hold you in high esteem. We wish you the very best of everything…. Best regards…."

—Bob.

In a letter dated January 22, 2009:

"Dear David and Elaine,

My two favorite people. I have patronly affection for both of you, as you are special people. You are in my prayers and God be with you."

—Bob

Cards to David:

"David,

You are a great man and I would always want you at my side if I were in a life and death situation. Of course, I would enjoy your fellowship at other times also. God be with you."

—Bob

"Dear David,

Whenever I had a tough assignment, I gave it to you. And you came through with flying colors. I have valued our friendship for nearly fifty years. You have always been an outstanding man and a credit to the Patrol. Best wishes."

—Bob

And one of the last conversations Dave had with Colonel Chiaramonte before the Colonel died:

> I went to see the Colonel. He was lying in bed and I held his hand.
>
> I said, "Colonel, thank you for all you did for me."
>
> He replied, "I gave you the dirtiest jobs and you always went."
>
> I said, "Yes, sir. I never wanted to disappoint you."
>
> "You never did," replied the Colonel. "I wish I had treated you better."

As Colonel Chiaramonte's health declined, Dave and I had many visits and conversations with him. In one conversation, there was the healing that came between mentor and trooper. The Colonel told me he protected Dave from the politics. He did not want him to have to go through what he went through. He loved Dave as a son, so being the father, he wanted to protect him.

In those last months, Dave and his mentor were able to heal and to say "I love you" and to let go. They were able to remember and tell stories together and to be thankful for life lived together on the Patrol.

Life Lesson

- We are to love and respect people, but not put them on a pedestal. Everyone is imperfect and has flaws. We admire and follow the good qualities in others and incorporate what we learn from others into our own lives.

Becoming the Major

"I had a very unique career in the Highway Patrol. One that nobody else will ever have."

David D. Sturtz began his Ohio State Highway Patrol career in 1957 as a Cadet Dispatcher at New Philadelphia. He sat desk, rode with troopers and studied the laws to prepare him for the Academy. He entered the 50th Academy Class at Hartman Farms in 1959 and graduated on June 26, 1959. His Unit number was 733. His first assignment was Lisbon, Post 15. It was here he met Merle Darrah, his coach and lifelong friend.

Within six months of graduating from the Academy, he received a call to be the PT instructor.

> When I got the call, I thought it was the guys at the post joking around with me, but then I realized this was real. I was to replace the guy I respected who was my legend on the highway patrol, Corporal Manly. If Manly said we were burning Atlanta, I would be cutting wick and be right behind him.

Dave was then severely injured in a car crash while on routine patrol. Dave recovered and was assigned to the Lancaster Post 23 in 1960. He continued to instruct at the Academy. Then Dave received a call from Colonel Chiaramonte: "I have a job for you in my home county, can you handle it?" Dave was promoted to Corporal on August 1, 1965.

As Dave would say, "When you get called by the head guy, you go."

Dave was assigned to the Ashtabula Patrol Post as Corporal and Assistant Post Commander. He was the youngest corporal and worked with guys who had many years on the patrol.

> *"Do not let anyone treat you as if you are unimportant*
> *because you are young."*
> *(1 Timothy 4:12, NCV)*

Dave recalled,

> I'd be sitting in on a meeting, and the older guys would say, "What does the young corporal have to say about this?" I always had an answer, and pretty soon they'd ask, "Dave, what do you think?" It took a while but I earned respect.

Then, Dave received his next call from Colonel Chiaramonte.

> It was like Mission Impossible. The Colonel would call if there was anything in the Patrol, any trouble. He would say, "You don't have to accept this. Only you and I will know."
>
> I replied, "You're calling me, then I'm going."

Dave was promoted to Sergeant on May 7, 1967. Dave was assigned to open a new post in Lebanon, the first new post in 20 years.

> Headquarters' staff set a five-year plan and goal for the Lebanon Post, and we met their numbers in seventeen months. I worked out of the Hamilton Post because Lebanon Post wasn't built yet. I met with my troopers and corporals and wasn't impressed. I got in my car and drove to Columbus. I didn't call ahead. I just showed up at Headquarters knocking on the Colonel's door. Miss B. (his secretary) said, "Sergeant, I don't think the Colonel can see you."
>
> I said, "I need to see him, will you help me?"
>
> Major Manly was aide-de-camp and told me "no!"
>
> "I need to see the Colonel." He made room for me.
>
> I stood in front of his desk. "What's going on?" he asked.
>
> "I just met with the folks you have given me. You've given me goals, but you have not given me good material."
>
> And the Colonel said, "You know what, Sturtz, you will do it. Go back to that post and make it work."
>
> "Yes sir." I made an about face, and out the door I went.
>
> I went back and called another meeting the next day. I said, "This is where we are. You don't know me, and I don't know you, but this is what we are going to do. If you don't want to be here or accept what we are going to do, leave now. I guarantee

you a transfer. I'll get you out of here, but if you stay, this is what we are going to do."

I had a plan, and they dove in. I worked with them. They worked. Most of them came on penalty (did something wrong.) One kept wrecking cars. Colonel Chiaramonte had faith in me. "You can do it. Make it work." I figured in my own mind that if he thinks I can do it, I'm going to do it. It took work. I lived at the post at first because my family was still in Ashtabula.

We shined them up. They had pride. I told them to wear their Stetsons all the time. "Wear them with pride, you are in command." They started to believe it, but it was work. I loved doing that. We made something out of nothing.

In 1968, Dave participated in shutting down inmate riots at the Ohio Penitentiary, the London Correctional Institute and the Lebanon Correctional Institute. On October 1, 1968, Dave was promoted to Staff Lieutenant and Assistant District Commander and assigned to Massillon District Headquarters. He was reassigned to the Wilmington District Headquarters Staff. Xenia Post had a drive-by shooting, and Dave was placed in charge of the on-scene situation. He was involved in stopping the Central State University riot and dealing with the dissidents and radicals. Dave was sent to Northwestern University's Traffic Institute and completed a nine-month training course in Traffic Police Administration, graduating on June 13, 1970. He was elected President of his class. When Dave returned to Ohio, he was temporarily assigned to the Academy and traveled around the state leading riot training. After Dave had completed the riot training, Colonel Chiaramonte asked for a report of the state of the Patrol.

> It is from excellent to terrible. District 1, give them to Michigan. It is terrible. No morale. It's sloppy. Captain is a nice guy, but not a leader.

Dave was assigned to Bucyrus Post for a short time and was promoted to Captain on October 19, 1970 and assigned to the Findlay District Headquarters as the Commander. Dave was assigned to the District he had assessed as the worst. It was in Findlay that he created the Obstacle Course. Details of the course are shared in another chapter.

In 1973, Dave was reassigned to the Ohio State Highway Patrol Academy as the Academy Commandant. This is a place where he thrived. He loved to teach and be a part of the new cadets' training and conditioning. Dr. Norris Lenahan was the Patrol doctor, having his office at the Academy.

> I admired Dr. Lenahan for his compassion, his honesty and his friendship. He had a great sense of humor. He was small in stature but a giant among the patrol. While I was Commandant of the Academy, boxing week was a very stressful, high anxiety and physically demanding week for each cadet. Dr. Lenahan would not only dispense medical remedies for black eyes, bruised arms, sore ribs, and bloody noses, but he would give advice on how they could have or should have protected themselves. It was always funny to me that some of the boxing information Dr. Lenahan gave never seemed to help the cadets. But it always made him feel good that he not only

medically helped them but felt he was giving advice to the next great fighter. I told Dr. Lenahan if his advice was so good, why was he still tending to so many bruised and battered cadets. He laughed and stated, "Maybe they haven't been hit hard enough to loosen the wax out of their ears so that they could better hear and use my advice."

In 1974, Dave was relieved from command of the Academy by the Colonel who assigned him.

I was out making a speech for the Colonel. It was boxing week at the Academy. One of the cadets was injured and had to have surgery to release pressure on the brain. One of our politicians was contacted by the family and the Colonel was contacted by the politician. The Colonel had to do something, so I was relieved of my command. I said, "I wasn't even on the reservation at the time." It didn't matter to the Colonel. I was in charge, and it was my responsibility. I could have pouted. I was moved by the guy who sent me. It hurt. I pouted for about thirty minutes. I had a new assignment and that was what I was going to do.

Dave was assigned as the Chief Recruiter for the State Highway Patrol with the directive to focus on minorities and women. He traveled the state as the spokesman and recruiter and did the job.

On April 7, 1975, Dave was promoted to the rank of Major by Colonel Frank Blackstone. Dave held the rank of Major for the rest of his Patrol career. He was a Major for nearly thirteen years. He held every position as Major: Bureau of Personnel, Bureau of Operations, Bureau of Technical Services, and Bureau of Inspections and Standards.

I served in every Headquarters position as Major. I was the longest serving major. Nearly thirteen years of my thirty-year career I was a Major. It will never happen again.

Therefore, the title "The Major" is fitting for David D. Sturtz.

Dave retired from the Ohio State Highway Patrol on January 16, 1988.

The Legend

In 1968, Dave was assigned to watch dissidents and radicals during this time of unrest in our country due to the Vietnam War and the racial tensions. Dave spent months in surveillance of Black Panther groups, the underground radicals, and the agitators on campuses. During this turmoil, he was all over the state. His face began to be recognized by these groups so he disappeared from Ohio for a year and went to Northwestern University's Traffic Institute. Dave continued to study about radicals and preparations needed to deal with this unrest. Here is what happened next:

> I came back from Northwestern with no assignment. I was at the Academy and Colonel Chiaramonte came into my dorm room and said, "I have a mission for you. I want you to go around the state—district to district—and train people in dealing with dissidents."
>
> I asked, "What do you want?"
>
> He said, "I'm going to leave that up to you."

Well, I put on a black jump suit. I got Ed
Centofante, the helicopter pilot. I got a big baton
and made some Molotov cocktails. Got all my
intelligence together and went to train people. I
threw tear gas on them and hit them with sticks. I
went to a rug place and got all their bamboo and
cut them into three-foot pieces and split them so
you could hit. I taught troopers how to use three-
foot sticks to hit and jab. I did this for ten weeks. I
went from 217 pounds to 190 pounds doing this
training.

And here is one of the reasons Dave was called the
Legend:

I was doing riot training. Being an athlete, you
wear a cup, a protective cup, for your groin area. I
had a magnesium cup, a metal cup. I was up on a
raised platform in front of a hundred male
troopers. I've got a three-foot stick and I'm
holding it in the middle. "This is how tough you
are going to be." Whack! I hit myself in the groin
and it clanged. I did it again and said, "We are
going into battle. You are superman with a cup,
and an idiot without one. Get a cup." The ones in
the back didn't know I had a cup. They couldn't
believe I would hit myself. It really impressed
them I was told later, and I got their attention. "If I
come out and give you a command, just do it or
I'll hit you with this stick."

Nobody on the State Highway Patrol had ever done
training like Dave did in 1969-70. One retiree shares his
memory of this training:

"You were a lieutenant holding a class concerning
the riots. You walked into the room wearing your

black jump suit and carrying your thirty-six-inch baton. You were talking and began striking yourself in the groin area. My thoughts were 'what kind of man is this, but I want to be like him.' You then told us to buy a cup to protect ourselves. You made a lasting positive impression on me from that point."

—Ernie Wilson

Here are a couple other retirees who share about "The Legend":

"You became a legend in your own time."

—Doug Wells

"I remember first hearing about Dave Sturtz, the iron man, the animal, the savage, the man who held the bar so high that to meet that level would be an amazing feat. You were and are highly respected, yet a bit feared if we could not meet your expectations, and your expectations are always high. That level of high expectations made our Patrol a stronger, healthier and better organization. You never let us down. Your whole career in the Patrol, you have been an example of strong leadership. People looked up to you. You always spoke with great authority and you commanded the utmost respect. We have yet to have another person be similar to a Dave Sturtz in the Patrol. In our Patrol history you will always be known as one-of-a-kind."

—Shel Senek

The Storyteller's Highway Patrol Stories

Dave loved to tell about his adventures on the Highway Patrol and people loved to hear him tell the stories. He became very animated as he shared and the listeners felt drawn into the stories. Reading the stories is not the same, but those who have heard Dave tell the stories will picture in their minds the memory of hearing Dave tell them. These are just a few of the many stories Dave told over the years. Remember, these are Dave's perception of what happened.

The "Honkey" Story

I was the post commander at Lebanon and Tom Rice was Corporal at Xenia. We met at Frisch's Restaurant in Xenia to organize self-defense training and baton usage to the Lebanon Correctional Officers. We were sitting at a table building our lesson plans when I received a call from Captain Carey, the District 8 Commander in Wilmington. He asked us to go out to Central State University, because something was going on out there. He told me to get in a car and go get some information.

We arrived at the campus. There was a lot of construction and a crowd near a dorm building forming into a riot. So, we parked our cars and we walked up. The students and the agitators saw us.

We heard, "Huhu."

I said, "What did they say?" So, we got closer.

"Huhu."

We can't understand what the words are. So, we finally move in where a girl yells out, "Kill Honkey."

And I looked over at Tom and said, "Whoever Honkey is, he is in big trouble."

All of a sudden, I realize, we are "honkey." It was the first time I ever heard that word. Michael Jackson didn't do the first moon walk dance; Tom Rice and I moved back out of there.

Then for the next three days, the Highway Patrol fought on Central State Campus. Two Lieutenants had a platoon, and Sergeant Sturtz, I had a reserve platoon. I had my Stetson and a three-foot baton. I saw the other platoons falling and at the time didn't realize they were slipping on the pavement because of their slick shoes.

We moved out. Tom Rice was in my platoon. The building had three stories, a roof and I'm there and Tom Rice screams, "Sturtz, move!"

And I leap ahead, and right behind me a grate from the street hits into the pavement. If it had hit me, it would have killed me. Tom did great.

We went inside, and Ralph Fussner is beside me, and we run up three flights of steps, and it's just me and Ralph. The rest of the platoon hasn't caught up yet. Something hits me in the chest, and I can't breathe. I'm thinking, "Did I get shot?"

But my adrenaline is so high. We are fighting and moving and finally get a break, and Ralph Fussner says, "Sarg, you OK?"

I said, "I hurt. It's hard to breathe."

He hands me a brass door knob. "That's what hit you." They threw it like a baseball. If it would have hit me in the head, it would have killed me.

We fought for three days. It was our first college campus riot.

The Chases

Dave loved to tell stories of his various chases on foot or in a car during his Highway Patrol days. He would become very animated. You began to think he was actually in the chase as he shared the story.

When I was stationed in Lancaster, I got a call on the radio that a prisoner had escaped while being transported to prison. The young guy had taken off on foot. As I was driving near the location, I saw the guy and he took off across a field. I pulled over, got out of my car and took off after the guy. My Stetson blew off. It's a hot late summer day, and I'm sweating. I'm running in my chuck boots, long sleeve wool shirt and wool pants. We are jumping over fences and across ditches and then the guy runs into a cornfield, and I take off after him. The corn is high, and I'm getting hit and cut by the branches. My shirt is all cut up and my skin is getting cut. But I keep running and finally we get out of the field. The kid doesn't have a shirt on and he's all bloody and I grab him. The deputy sheriff pulls up. They handcuff him. The guy looks at them and says, "Who is that guy?" I think he was more scared of me than getting caught. He was all bloody and out of breath.

I had cuts all over my face and hands. The deputy and patrol guys ask, "What happened to you?"

When they found my car and where I had started chasing the guy, it was eleven miles away. I kept up. The kid couldn't believe an "old man" like me could do what I did, but I caught him.

One of the youth in our Sunday School class asked Dave how fast he had ever driven in a patrol car on the road.

I was out driving in Fairfield County and at a crossroad when "zoom," a black BMW flew by. I turned on my little bubble light on top of my cruiser and took off after the car down Refugee Road. This was back in the 1960's before anything was on Refugee. He kept going and I looked down and was going 120 mph. My cruiser started shaking. When I finally caught the guy, he said he was late to meet his friend.

The youth always asked Dave if he ever shot anyone. He would say,

I had to pull my gun out, but I never shot anyone. I almost shot a deputy sheriff once. Several prisoners had escaped and they thought they might be hiding in old barns. So, the patrol and sheriff department were working together, and we went out as teams. I had a deputy sheriff with me. We stopped at this old barn. I handed him my shotgun to be on the watch outside, while I searched the barn. I slowly worked my way into the barn, searching through the old straw and equipment. Then I heard the barn door open. I pulled out my gun and my finger was on the trigger when I heard, "Hey, how do you get the safety latch off this shotgun." It was the deputy. I yelled at him to get out of the barn, and I slowly put my gun away.

I ran out of that barn and yelled at that deputy. "I almost shot you. Get in the car and don't get out again." I took him back to the post and said, "I'll go out on my own."

The Search

When I was stationed at Lancaster, there was an escapee from jail. We were all given our assignments. I was to search the area near Carroll. There was a huge road culvert that they thought could be a hiding place.

It was cold and dark out in late November. I parked my car, got my flashlight and headed down the embankment. I shined my little flashlight inside but couldn't see anything. I started down inside walking through the water and rocks when my boot got stuck between the rocks. I fell and my flashlight went flying in the opposite direction. I couldn't get my foot unstuck. There was mud and cold water and ice all around me. I kept pulling. I had no radio to call for help. I yelled, and traffic covered up my voice. I started to think, "I could freeze and die down here." I kept pulling and finally my foot came out of my boot.

I crawled out of there and walked back to my car with my now frozen sock flapping. I was so cold and shaking that I couldn't get my key into the lock of the car. Finally, I did, and I turned on the car and turned the heater on high. I radioed the post that the culvert was clear. I didn't know I was stuttering because of being so cold.

I made it back to the post. I walked in with my sock still frozen and flapping. Captain said, "What happened to you?"

The Old Preacher

I was stationed in Lisbon in 1959. I was out on patrol and stopped this rat-trap truck. It had bald tires, no turn signals, broken headlight, no muffler and I think it was held together with rust. I arrested the guy for an unsafe vehicle and waited for the wrecker to come and get it. The old guy had been hunting and was dressed in old hunting clothes that were dirty, with an old threadbare hat and coat.

He was polite and respectful. He asked if I could take him home. I told him that I was not allowed to. He said, "I need to get home tonight. I have dinner for my family."

I looked in the back of his truck, and he had skinned squirrels and rabbits. I thought, "I'm not putting those dead animals in my clean car."

"Please, sir. My family is expecting me tonight."

I finally agreed and opened up my trunk, and we put all those dead, smelly animals in there.

Then he said, "I need to ask another favor, sir. Can we take my dog? I can't leave him here and I need him for hunting."

I looked inside his truck and there was his old dirty hound dog. I got a blanket from the trunk, and we put the dog in the back seat of my car. The dog stunk. The old guy smelled and all those dead animals. All I could think was "what if my Sergeant sees me? I'll never get this smell out of my car."

Well, I took him home. I went down old country roads, curved around into a mud and gravel road that ended at an old ratty shack. When I pulled in, a lady and three little kids came out on the porch. The old guy thanked me for taking him, his dog and the animals home so he could feed his family. My car smelled for weeks. I scrubbed it out, but it still smelled.

About two months later, I was in a car accident and was in the Salem City Hospital for weeks in traction. One day, the nurse came in and said, "There is an old black preacher out here who wants to see the Patrolman."

I said, "I don't know who that would be, but let him come in."

In walks this black gentleman, in a threadbare suit with the collar worn out, a necktie and old white shirt. He is carrying a big worn leather Bible. He said, "I don't know if you remember me." I did; it was that old guy I took home with his hound dog and dead animals. "I saw in the paper that you were in an accident. You were so kind to me that I came to pray with you." The guy had hitchhiked across two counties to get to the hospital. He was a preacher. He prayed this prayer over me and then left. I couldn't believe that he would come all that way to pray with a person who had arrested him.

There are so many more stories that could be shared in this book. Some of you who are reading this now have stories and memories that come to mind. Remember them and share them with others. The gift of storytelling needs to continue to each generation.

Life Lesson

- Tell your stories. Learn from the past and listen to the stories of those who came before you and learn. Laugh and enjoy, too!

CHAPTER 5

LEADERSHIP

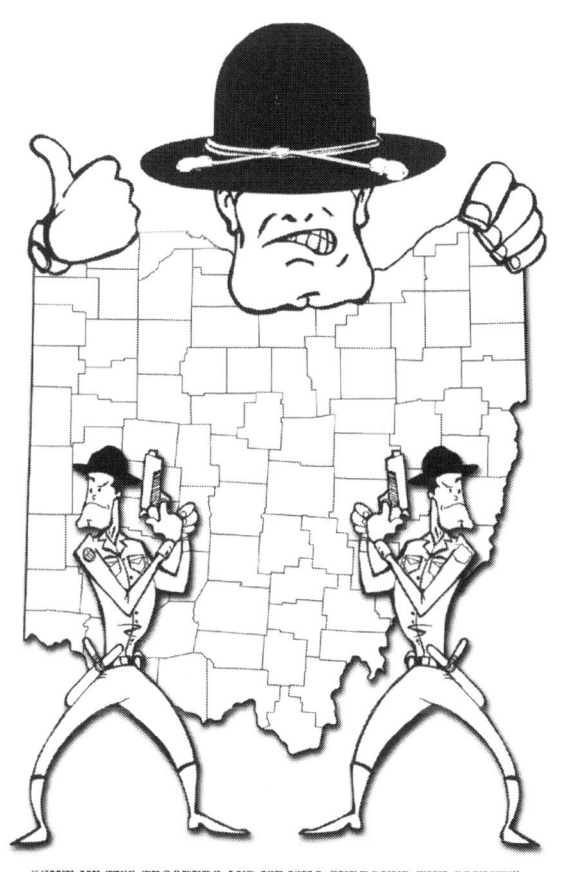

"GIVE ME TWO TROOPERS AND WE WILL SURROUND THE COUNTY"

The Leader

This Chapter is filled with the words of David D. Sturtz on leadership. Many of the words are taken from the numerous speeches Dave shared throughout the state and in the courses on leadership he taught throughout his career. Dave led by example. He believed and lived the words he spoke.

His brother, Ken, describes Dave's leadership:

> Dave's character was burnished over the years, and as he grew older he grew wiser as he developed undeniable leadership qualities. As a young athlete he played quarterback on the football team, catcher on the baseball team and point guard on the basketball team, all positions requiring leadership skills. As a member of the Ohio State Patrol, Dave continued to hone his leadership skills. It would be easy to say Dave was a "natural" leader, but it is also true he was dedicated to continued progress toward effective leadership qualities.

Throughout his entire law enforcement career, Dave continued to develop and refine his leadership qualities. He tried to instill the basic values of a good leader into those he taught and with whom he worked. One does not just deem themselves a leader. To be a leader, other people must be willing to follow. I share with you some of the comments from letters of people who followed Dave's leadership.

> "When Dave taught at the Academy, all of the troopers who were in his riot class training would

have followed him to the end. He was, in our eyes, a person one could describe as a born leader. His confidence and personal bearing and friendly demeanor were second to none."

—S.A. Stark

"Major Sturtz was always direct and spoke with conviction. He never belittled me. He instructed me to do better in actions and decision making. I appreciated that he took the time to listen to my side without interrupting as I told it. Major Sturtz was one person in authority I would have followed anywhere with no questions asked. I valued his leadership."

—Monte Shewman

"The leadership you gave to us still stands and still helps us daily. We knew to be right, and you would back us up."

—R.A. Smith

"I remember as a cadet, he came in to our class and discussed the honor of being a Patrolman (later changed to Trooper). The one specific thing he said that has forever stuck with me was 'You give me one other Patrolman and we can surround this Academy.' It truly impressed upon me that we could do anything. He ranks as the best officer that I had dealings with in my twenty-five-year career. I knew that if I ever had to go battle, I wanted him as my leader."

—Thomas Moline

"At the first Legend Valley Rock concert, we were all summoned to a volunteer fire department from our positions when the Major explained that we could be in a tight situation. He told us to get our riot gear ready and be ready to confront the crowd. I must admit the Major gave quite a stirring speech, and I would have followed him right off a cliff had he decided that's where we needed to go. Of all the leaders that I ever had on the patrol in thirty years, I must say that the Major had the most charisma of anyone I ever met."

—Mark Malcom

"Dave saw in leaders their weaknesses but he didn't use it for personal gain. He found ways behind the scene to fill the hole from the weaknesses."

—Gene Archer

"I was assigned as an instructor at the Academy when Dave was the Commander of the Training Academy. He was always positive and approachable. If you had an issue or problem, you were not hesitant to seek his advice or assistance. His actions, appearance, personality and physical fitness set the example for the academy staff, cadets and all officers attending classes there. He never asked anyone to do anything that he would not do himself."

—Rob Hartsell

In his leading, Dave was always teaching. He had the ability to see the bigger picture and recognize gifts and talents within a person. His leadership helped others to gain confidence and to excel in their jobs and careers. Dave was serving as he led by encouraging and demanding excellence which produced strength of character.

"Preach the Good News. Be ready at all times,
and tell people what they need to do.
Tell them when they are wrong.
Encourage them with great patience and careful teaching."
(2 Timothy 4:2, NCV)

Life Lesson

- Lead by example.

Leadership Philosophy

The qualities Dave attributed to a leader were *"character, ethics, integrity, honesty, and solid virtues."*

"Push, Pull or get the hell out of the way." This was one of Dave's main leadership statements. This is how he explained it in several speeches:

> Push, pull or get the hell out of the way, we need you here. Push, pull or get the hell out of the way because we have important things to do. Do something or get out of the way so someone else can work. Be a doer and take the necessary action. Don't be afraid of being in charge.

"Give me two good troopers and we can surround the county. There is nothing we couldn't handle together." Dave believed in the organization and the training, and because of that knowledge he and a trooper could handle whatever happened.

"The greatest way to ever influence anyone's behavior is role modeling and there is no exception." Dave's leadership style was to lead by example. He never asked anyone to do something he did not do. When he was leading a

group in the obstacle course, he ran with each group. When he led a battalion in a riot, Dave was the first in line. When he was Academy Commandant, he ran with the cadets.

"You work until the work is done. It doesn't matter your rank, you lead by example." When given an assignment, Dave always completed the task with a positive attitude. No task was too small and there was no job that you couldn't make challenging. *"One person working towards a goal is better than ninety-nine thinking about it."*

Dave was adamant that leaders had to be themselves and use their God given gifts and talents to lead in their own style. Style though was not as important as the basic qualities of honesty, character, and integrity. Dave was always his own person.

> We can all learn from the successful and effective experiences of others. But there is no way you can be successful trying to be like someone you are not.

Dave learned from his failures and mistakes, which made him a strong leader.

> No one is immune from making mistakes and using poor judgment; however, it is how you recover by using skills and abilities of an effective leader. You will earn the respect and admiration of those who depend upon you because you won't allow yourself to fail or let them fail.

Dave believed character was the foundation of a good leader.

Adversity is a crossroad that makes every person choose one of two paths—character or compromise. Every time people choose character they become stronger, even if the choice brings negative consequences. Your character determines who you are. Who you are determines what you see. And what you see determines what you do. That's why you cannot separate a leader's character from his actions.

A leader needed strong communication skills.

Developing excellent communication skills is absolutely essential to an effective and influential leader. The leader must be able to share knowledge, ideas and to transmit a sense of urgency and enthusiasm to others. If a leader cannot get a message across clearly and motivate others to act on it, then having a message, no matter how good it is, doesn't even matter. A leader must get things done through others. Therefore, the leader must have the ability to inspire and motivate, guide, give direction and listen. It is only through skillful communication that the leader is able to cause others to accept the cause and to work toward implementing it.

Regarding trust, Dave stated,

Trust is the bedrock and foundation of leadership. You don't build trust by talking about it. You build it by achieving results with integrity, always in a manner that displays real personal regard for all the people with whom you work.

If you want to locate the leader in your midst, just identify the person you can trust the most to get things done no matter what and with no excuses. They are hidden in plain view doing what leaders do—their jobs and a little bit more, sometimes a lot more.

Dave highlighted the need for integrity.

Above all else workers want a leader who is known for honesty, one with strong character and someone whom they can trust. If your word is good as gold and your actions prove it true, others hearing what you say know that they can depend on you. This goes both ways from the leaders to the followers and from the followers to the leaders.

Regarding courage, Dave believed, "The greatest element of leadership is courage."

"Be alert. Continue strong in the faith.
Have courage and be strong. Do everything in love."
(1 Corinthians 16:13-14, NCV)

Life Lesson

* The foundation of a leader is character. A leader communicates and learns from failure.

Leadership

The following words are Dave's view of leadership that he shared in speeches over his career. In speaking with law enforcement, he said,

Enforce the laws that are violated. Do this with honesty and deal with the facts. Be fair and impartial. Don't have double or triple standards, but have one professional standard for all. The police profession must commit itself to fighting for and preserving the highest ethical standards for all members of our society that we protect.

Don't just sit on the front lines of society. People want you across that line, deep into enemy territory, utilizing all your physical, mental, ethical and moral strengths. It is the right thing to do. Moreover, it is the only thing to do. No other profession is more regulated and scrutinized than the law enforcement community. We must continue to earn and maintain the trust of those we police.

If you want to be an effective leader and influence those around you, you must be committed.

True commitment inspires and attracts people. It shows them that you have principles and convictions. They will believe in you only if you believe in yourself and in your cause.

There are two scriptures that remind me of my time on the Highway Patrol and as Inspector General. The first one is Proverbs 20:12 (RSV), that says, "The hearing ear and the seeing eye, the Lord has made them both." And from Isaiah 40:31 (RSV), "They who wait upon the Lord shall renew their strength. They shall mount up with wings as eagles. They shall run and not be weary. They shall walk and not faint." The Ohio State Highway Patrol and the Inspector General's Office are the "hearing ears" and the "seeing eyes" of government. We have the strength. We have the wings of eagles. We will run and not be weary of our tasks. We will walk through any complex problems and not faint.

> You must know where you have been to get to where you want to be in the future.

Dave spoke twice as the Commencement Speaker at the State Highway Patrol Academy. Here are a few of his words to the 141st Graduating Class:

> Your race has begun. Whether you are a sprinter, plodder or walker, finish the race by being honest, having a sense of urgency, paying attention to all of the details, being a team player, always being a professional, adapting to everything around you, staying self-disciplined, performing your duties to be successful, and always protecting yourself and your brothers' and sisters' lives by always being aware of what is in your environment.
>
> You are part of something bigger than yourself, but without your individual efforts and you working as a team, traditions die, oak trees are cut down and organizations fade from everyone's memory. This will not happen to the Ohio State Highway Patrol because you are now going to interject your energy, your brain power, your enthusiasm, and you will make sure that nothing stops the momentum of who we are, who you are and what the Ohio State Patrol has stood for over the years.

Dave ended most of his speeches with this challenge from John Wesley. (These words are attributed to John Wesley but are not found directly in any of his sermons.)

> I would like to leave you with a challenge. It is a challenge that has its roots over two hundred years ago. It was first spoken and practiced by John Wesley, Founder of the Methodist Church. These words, I believe, are as viable and valid today as when Wesley first gave this rule of life. He stated:

"Do all the good you can, by all the means you can, by all the ways you can, in all the places you can, in all the lives you can, to all of the people you can, as long as you can."

I conclude this chapter on leadership with two statements written by Dave with his unique flair and choice of words.

You just don't go to bed one night and wake up the next morning pregnant. You've got to be involved. You must have knowledge. You must be doing something you shouldn't be doing. If you are wrong, admit it, change, and then do the right thing.

Can you survive an ethics frisk, back against the wall, hands over your head, the cruel light of day focused on your personal or professional life? What is there that brings you down or elevates you to trusted status? This is only a frisk. Can you also pass an exhaustive investigation of your personal and professional life by the media or anyone else?

Dave was a natural leader who continued to sharpen and hone his leadership skills through his professional careers. He lived what he believed. He made mistakes, but he learned from them. He encouraged, inspired, pushed, and challenged others to be their best and do their best.

Life Lesson

- Be a leader. Be ethical, honest, and trustworthy, with integrity and character. A sense of humor and love for people makes a great leader who is likable too.

CHAPTER 6

THE INSPECTOR GENERAL

The Creation of the Office

"In the beginning God created the heavens and the earth.
The earth was without form and void..."
(Genesis 1:1-2, RSV)

The Office of Inspector General for the State of Ohio was created by Executive Order under Governor Richard Celeste. The press release dated June 7, 1988 read in part,

> The Inspector General, appointed by the Governor, will examine and investigate and make recommendation to prevent and detect wrongful acts in the Governor's Office and the agencies of state government.

Dave had retired from the Ohio State Highway Patrol on January 16, 1988 to be home with his wife, Iris, who was battling cancer. Dave read about this newly created position and said, "I could do that." He was encouraged to apply, but he said, "They won't touch a guy like me." Dave was contacted by the deputy chief of staff whom he had met at a previous function. Dave finally applied and was interviewed by the Governor. It was narrowed down to two candidates. On Wednesday, August 3, 1988 at 6:15 p.m., Dave received a phone call from the Governor's Chief of Staff congratulating him on being appointed the First Inspector General of Ohio.

According to Dave's notes, he was given the program: "Press conference with the Governor who will read charge letter with duties and make a few statements concerning my background. Then I will make a few comments. Then Q's & A's. 7th Floor office—new state office tower."

Dave was named Inspector General at the news conference on August 4, 1988. During the question time, a question was asked of the Governor, Dave recalls:

> The Governor turned to me and said, "I'm not going to tell you how to run your office."
>
> I said, "I appreciate that." And I smiled at the Governor and everyone laughed.

Dave officially began as the first Inspector General for the State of Ohio on August 8, 1988 or as he always said, *"On 8-8-88."* Dave was given a small empty office in the Statehouse. The first day he was working in it, someone came in and told him he had to leave, that he was using Mrs. Celeste's office. He said, "She will have to use another space, this is mine." He continued working out of that office until his space was ready on the 29th floor of the Riffe building. "I had a desk, a legal pad and a pen, and I began working."

The first week, Dave met with the Editorial Boards of all the major Ohio newspapers. Dave hit it head on. He knew they were going to question his independence. Dave told all the newspapers,

> I have gone on record that I am independent. You will have to take my word for it until some time goes by to judge my performance. I have certain things I want to accomplish, and if I can't, I will walk away.

He also told the newspapers, "We will go with whatever is given to us by the newspapers and the public and get involved in that way."

Dave became known as "The Watchdog" of State Government. Dave liked that title. Dave spoke honestly and straightforwardly to the newspaper editorial boards, to which they were not accustomed. Dave was very vocal that he was not a politician. He was hired to investigate.

> I'm here and I want to do this job. I think I will enjoy the challenge of setting up an arm of government and making it into something.

Dave loved a challenge. He enjoyed the freedom to develop a project, program, training and now a new office. He always said, "I created the Office of Inspector General from a piece of paper."

Dave put together a plan. After visiting all the major newspapers, he contacted the three Inspector Generals in the states who at that time had the position – Massachusetts, Pennsylvania, and New York. He visited each Inspector General and gathered information in how they were organized, how they conducted investigations, their staffing and reporting. He analyzed all of this information and used what was beneficial for Ohio. Dave wrote the procedures for handling allegations and investigations.

The Executive Order allowed Dave to hire two investigators and one office staff. He hired Jack Alsop as Deputy Inspector General and David Bosley as legal investigator. Janet Journey Wise was hired as the Administrative Assistant. Later Eva Wolfram was hired as additional secretarial assistance. In time, Jack Alsop and David Bosley moved to other positions in government, and Dave hired Richard Emmons and Rick Tilton.

Janet Journey describes the creation of the office and working with the Inspector General:

> When I met Dave Sturtz, I was being interviewed by him for the position of Administrative Assistant for this newly created office. The meeting was in the newly built, mostly vacant Riffe Office Tower. Off in the corner of an empty floor stood a desk, a couple of chairs, and a file cabinet and that's where the interview took place. What struck me most about him during this first meeting was his confidence and excitement for the challenge ahead as he explained the details of his vision for the office. Also apparent was his dogged determination to uphold the ethics required in order to make the office as revered as he believed it should. I knew that for a man who possessed such confidence, strength, and drive, there would be nothing less than high expectations and complete success. With nothing but desks, chairs, empty file cabinets and an Executive Order in hand, our small group set out on the adventure of a lifetime, with Dave at the helm. Within a very short time, directives were prepared, and cases began to roll into the office. Under his guidance, he steered the ship into uncharted waters, investigating waste, fraud, abuse and corruption within state government, determined to be non-partisan, fair and right which was everything he stood for.

> The other members of the office seemed confident and at ease each day with the tasks at hand. However, for me there were some people of position and power that I felt hesitant to address and/or approach; or tasks that were well beyond

my previous experience and seemed daunting to say the least. Dave was always reassuring and confident of my skills during those times, pledging his support without waiver. He would tell me if I made a decision based on the best information and judgment I had, he would stand behind me. That's the type of courage and inspiration his support instilled within me. We had long conversations about life that included strategy, ethics, emotions, thoughts and ideas. I handled office matters and made decisions that related to the daily tasks, earning his respect and trust. I couldn't imagine a greater reward in my life or career!

Eva Wolfram shares about her experience working in the Inspector General's Office:

David Sturtz was a man of honor, an example of courage and strength. The opportunity to have worked in the office of The Ohio Inspector General was amazing. I was quite nervous about interviewing for the secretary position. During the interview, I was impressed with I. G. Sturtz. He was professional, yet personable. He offered me the job, and I was excited to put it mildly. In casual moments, I enjoyed listening to his stories. His values were unquestionable. He was a 'hero' of sorts, restoring my faith in the goodness of people. He was strong and forthright and determined to attack corruption, no matter who was involved. He served the State of Ohio with honesty and dedication. He was a Godly man and a role model.

The five of them, Dave's total staff the entire time as Inspector General, investigated fraud, waste, corruption and abuse in the Executive Branch of Government. They were always busy.

Dave loved the challenge. His years on the State Highway Patrol prepared him for this next step.

Life Lesson

- Gather information from others who have gone before you, but create your own plan and go.

The General

"Do not be conformed to this world
but be transformed by the renewal of your mind,
that you may prove what is the will of God,
what is good and acceptable and perfect."
(Romans 12:2, RSV)

Dave *"eagerly"* accepted the challenge of being the State "Watchdog" against wrongdoing. Dave had no political connections. He was independent and had nothing to prove. He already had a thirty-year career in the State Highway Patrol. He had earned the respect of the Patrol and those he served. He was known for his integrity. Dave was willing to serve again, but also willing to walk away.

This combination truly made him the appropriate person to step into the fray of unethical practices, illegal political activity and the fraud, waste and abuse in government. Dave did not owe anybody anything and was not afraid to step on toes. Dave said, "I don't have to be popular or liked, I just need to do my job."

When Dave was interviewed after accepting the position, he said, "For thirty years I have reached out for responsibility and obligation. You have got to risk failure to succeed. I will not back away from that."

Dave accepted the challenge to be impartial and independent. In the midst of political corruption, bribes, fraud, abuse and illegal activity, Dave remained true to who he was. Dave stood firm on his foundation of values and principles. He maintained his integrity, honesty and character even when accused. As he said, "I stayed above the fray."

Dave was proud, honored and humbled to be the first Inspector General—"To be the first and nobody else can say that." He was proud that the Inspector General Office began with a piece of paper—an Executive Order—and within two years it became part of state law. It was because of his independence and willingness to ferret out wrongdoing and his ethical practices that the office became state law—House Bill 588.

Dave set the standard. He wasn't given much to start the office. He was given a directive, eventually a budget of $300,000 and finally, an office. Dave didn't hide or wait for direction. He used his God-given gifts and organized, hired staff, talked with people and got the word out that the Inspector General's Office was open for business. The newspapers even published his office address and telephone number. Besides meeting with other State Inspector Generals, Dave contacted all the state agencies of Ohio to share about the Inspector General's Office. He connected with law enforcement. Dave contacted all the state agencies within the Executive Branch and all cabinet members to inform them of the Office and what it did.

Working with other state agencies gave the Inspector General's Office additional support. Dave always said, "We are small but mighty." He did not try to do everything himself but relied on other agencies to assist. Dave remained independent. He learned to let criticism roll off of him and just do his job. He knew the system but was not part of the political games. He spent hours figuring out the connections. It was intriguing to him. It became like a puzzle to put the pieces together.

Dave said, "I've not pleased everybody, but I don't have to please anybody. I do what I think is right."

One of the low points in the first two years as Inspector General was the accusation of being a racist. Dave denied the allegations by presenting the facts—78% of the primary cases involved whites. Dave was hurt, but it did not influence his judgment or movement forward on his investigations.

The independence of Inspector General David D. Sturtz was evident when he was reappointed by the next Governor from the other political party, Governor Voinovich. In the second term, Voinovich did not reappoint Dave. Many of the newspapers supported his reappointment but stated Dave may have been doing too good of a job uncovering corruption and violations in the Executive Branch. Dave gained the support from previous legislators who did not think he would remain independent. When they saw that he had the same energy in investigations in both administrations, they recognized his true independence.

Dave remained impartial, unbiased and independent through his career as Inspector General. He became known to many as *"The General"* because he was the first who set the standard and also set the bar high. Dave never compromised his values and ethics. He proved you can work in the midst of politicians and not be influenced by them nor corrupted by those who are doing wrong. He also proved that there are good, strong, ethical people who work in state government.

Life Lesson

- Do your job. Do what is right. Stand your ground and do not let others influence you to do wrong.

The Investigator

"Test everything, hold fast what is good,
and abstain from every form of evil."
(1 Thessalonians 5:21-22, RSV)

Within four months of the creation of the Inspector General's Office, Dave had opened four major investigations and had dealt with ten complaints in which he worked with agencies to take the needed course of action. Within two years of being established, the Inspector General office became state law, and Dave and his small staff had completed over one hundred investigations. The need for the office was confirmed.

Dave was a fact seeker. He began to receive complaints in every possible way. He received letters, phone calls, slips of paper under his door, tips from the cleaning staff, leads from newspaper articles and so many other ways. He always followed up. He would meet people who were fearful for their jobs at different locations throughout the city and even around the state.

> *"Truth will continue forever,*
> *but lies are only for a moment."*
> *(Proverbs 12:19, NCV)*

Dave stood by each report and investigation. He signed off on everything that was completed and released from the office. Dave took full responsibility for the office. He only dealt in facts in the reports. If he could not substantiate a charge, he stated it was unsubstantiated. He did not make up things that were not found. Everything was grounded in the truth. Dave investigated whatever came through his door whether the complaint was at the lowest level of state government or was in the Governor's Office.

Dave's friend and former Director of the Secret Service, John Magaw, shares his view of Dave as Inspector General:

> David's strength of character was tested when, as the Ohio Inspector General, he found wrongdoing in very high places. The investigations that followed were very complete and detailed and did corroborate specific violations of law and ethics. Dave weathered the political pressure and moved forward with censorship and prosecution. He

suspected that doing the right thing would cost him his job. No matter, Dave proceeded.

Inspector General Sturtz knew a plethora of information. He never shared it, leaked it or used it for personal gain. He kept it to himself. That was his integrity. He never kept quiet, though about wrong. He stood up for what was right even if it would cost him his job. Therefore, in this chapter I will not be sharing about individual cases. From one of the investigative reports, Dave said,

> Examining the problems in this agency was similar to dealing with a many-headed hydra. As we looked at one problem area, the problem under examination would usually give rise to the discovery of several more problems which demanded our attention, examination and evaluation.

This happened for Dave in most of his investigations. He would start with one complaint and, while investigating, he would discover other problems and issues that needed to be investigated. Sometimes he would stop with the initial complaint and write his report. He would then write a letter to the Director about other issues that the Director needed to address within his/her agency.

The investigations involved a variety of cases. Dave investigated employee misconduct, mismanagement in agencies, abuse of time reports, filing false documents, conflicts of interest, contract violations, misuse of funds, bribery and list goes on. Wherever the investigation led, Dave followed the paper trail.

Each year as Inspector General, Dave and his office staff created an Annual Report. In the first one in 1989, Dave wrote these words in his introduction letter:

> The Office of State Inspector General has had an immediate impact on those things that disrupted the normal flow of what was expected within the executive branch of government. This office has dedicated itself to the responsibility and obligation of investigating fraud, waste, abuse and corruption. Countless hours have been expended in investigating valid, legitimate complaints. This office has gained a reputation for quick and precise action once called upon to investigate allegations of wrongdoing. It is felt that the creation of this office was definitely in the best interest of those we serve, the citizens of the State of Ohio.

Serving the citizens of Ohio was Dave's main focus. Each year the office received over one hundred complaints. The office gained the reputation of being trustworthy and it would take action. Employees of the State of Ohio felt they could trust Mr. Sturtz with their information and more people began to share concerns and information.

Being an investigator was a gift Dave had and used in his law enforcement career. But Dave knew trust was the key. If people didn't trust him, he would get no information.

Life Lesson

- Be honest. Build trust. Do what is right no matter what.

Tenure

"My son, keep sound wisdom and discretion;
let them not escape from your sight."
(Proverbs 3:21, RSV)

When Dave was not re-appointed for Governor Voinovich's second term because the Governor wanted a "fresh perspective," Dave said,

> I hope people will say that I was honest, that I was forthright and I didn't dodge any bullets that came in this door. We were fair and impartial.
>
> I feel like I've done my job very well for six years. He's made a change, and I'll go do something else with my life.
>
> I walked in here as an independent guy, and the day I leave I'll walk out an independent.
>
> We research, we investigate, we put out a factual report and that's how it is. If that upsets people, so be it.

During Dave's six and a half years as Inspector General, he received over six hundred complaints. He was always busy, and never turned down information. His great recall assisted him in pulling out facts and bits of information received in the past into current investigations.

In a speech Dave gave shortly after not being re-appointed, he summarized his tenure:

> I served in this position from August 8, 1988 until January 6, 1995. In my six and a half years as the Inspector General, many complex case investigations were handled. This was under both

a Democratic and a Republican administration. The work never ceased. The office was empowered to subpoena and place people under oath. The charge to me contained in the August 4, 1988 directive, read in part,

> *I expect the office of Inspector General to be an impartial and independent office, which will respond quickly and decisively to allegations of misconduct involving employees of state government. As the Inspector General, it is your duty and obligation to ensure that these expectations are fulfilled.*

In my entire tenure as the Inspector General, I did not deviate nor did I allow any of my staff to deviate from this charge. Whatever came in the door, wherever it led, regardless of whom it involved, our mission was to bring the waste, fraud, abuse and corruption to light.

Since my departure from the office, there have been numerous editorials and articles written and comments made from both sides of the isle and the one thing that is made very clear is that the Office of Inspector General is an important and much needed office in the realm of State Government. I was very proud to be the first Inspector General and to have set standards that are very high.

Dave returned home after the end of his Inspector General career but kept a close watch on the appointive process of his successor. He continued to read the newspapers and keep his opinions to himself. That is until April 7, 1995 when he wrote Governor Voinovich and shared his letter with seven newspapers. Dave had given his all to create the Office of Inspector General, and he wanted it to remain independent from the Governor's Office and to continue in the same high standard of ethics. He wanted it to move forward, but he was heartbroken to see what was happening. Here are a couple of excerpts from Dave's letter:

> In just three short months your administration has undone six and a half years of hard labor to keep politics out of that office. The words independent, fair and impartial were and are extremely important for that office to uphold.

> I am truly saddened and angered by what has been allowed to happen to a once respected, feared and professional office that the people could count on taking action.

For Dave it was like a death. He had sacrificed and created an office to serve the citizens of Ohio, to be a voice of hope and to fight the evils of government, and now he felt it was compromised. And he needed to take a stand.

Life Lesson

- Not everybody has the same high standards you do. You have no control over those who follow you. You still do your best and don't compromise your principles.

CHAPTER 7

PHYSICAL TRAINING

The Love of Sports

Dave loved sports. His favorite to play was whatever was in season while in high school. He loved to watch football on TV. His favorite pro football team was the Cleveland Browns, and his favorite all time player was Otto Graham. Dave enjoyed watching Ohio State Football because his Uncle Karl played for Ohio State. In basketball his favorite pro team was the Boston Celtics because of Larry Bird. He enjoyed the hustle and "never give up" attitude of Larry Bird. He felt connected to Larry Bird in attitude toward the game.

Dave enjoyed watching his children, Gretchen and Craig, play high school sports. He was one of those intense parents. His daughter, Gretchen states, "He was very vocal. I could hear him from the stands. He would speak up if the refs called something he did not agree on. He was a great supporter." He was more laid back but always into the game with his grandsons, Chris and O'Shay. You always knew Dave Sturtz was at the game and intensely watching the game.

In high school, Dave was the quarterback in football, the point guard in basketball, and the catcher in baseball. He was the leader for the team. Through these experiences, Dave developed his leadership skills and ability to work well with others. Dave remembered every score of his high school football career, who he played against and the details of many of the games. It was in his blood. But as he matured, he became aware of the deeper meaning of sports.

> I enjoyed all of the athletic games because it gave me a chance to compete, to lead and to be part of a team effort. Playing sports gave me the basics to be the man I am to this day.

Sports were more than just games with winners and losers. They were events that developed Dave's leadership skills, team work, and working toward a goal together. Dave loved the competitiveness of sports. He competed against others, but also against himself to better himself and set higher goals to attain. Dave was built like an athlete. His appearance was tall, muscular, and as he said, his mom called him "ruggedly handsome."

When Dave's son, Craig, was playing soccer in 1975, Dave went to the organizational meeting as a parent. Teams were chosen at this time, and a group of little boys was not chosen for any team. Here's what happened next:

> One of the coaches came up to me and said, "I need you to coach these boys who are left."
>
> I said, "No, I am here to watch my son play. He's over there on that team."
>
> The coach insisted, "If you don't coach them, they don't get to play."
>
> I looked at those snot nosed kids, tears running down their faces. Nobody wanted them. So finally, I agreed. I got those boys together, "Boys, we are tough. We can play and win this championship."
>
> The boys whined and cried that nobody wanted them and they didn't know how to play. I said, "I don't want to see any tears. We can do this. You are tough."

It took a while to get them together. None of those kids knew how to play. I didn't know soccer, but we practiced. I made them run and kick and we played. Pretty soon they won a game and then another. They started to believe in themselves. We were in the championship game. At half time, the boys started to complain about the referee. I told them, "Go wipe your nose on somebody else's knee. We are here to play." We won the championship with a group of reject kids that nobody wanted.

Dave was able to take a group of little boys who had no confidence and make them into champions. It was his leadership and love for the underdog that made it possible, and also his competitive nature. Those boys came to respect their coach, and it made a difference in their lives.

Sports prepared Dave for life, for his careers and guided him in his focus and ability to work for an organization.

Life Lesson

- Sports are more than games played on a field. They are part of the development and growth of an individual.

Personal Fitness

"You should know that your body is a temple
for the Holy Spirit who is in you.
You have received the Holy Spirit from God.
So you do not belong to yourselves,
because you were bought by God for a price.
So honor God with your bodies."
(1 Corinthians 6:19-20, NCV)

Dave loved practice in high school. He couldn't wait for workouts and even enjoyed "two-a-days" in football season. All through his childhood, he played outside and played hard. He ran all over town, and then later biked all over town. He ran to school and ran home for lunch and then ran back to school. Running came natural to Dave.

Playing three sports in high school kept him in great shape. Then he went to the University of Cincinnati and played football for two years which kept him working out and running all year around. He was ready to play softball in any league over the summers.

When Dave began his career on the Highway Patrol, he was in great physical condition. The physical training at the academy was like "recess" to him. It came naturally to him, and he loved it. Dave ran every day for years, running up to nine or ten miles daily. He would run on his lunch hour when he worked at the Highway Patrol Academy. He ran with the cadets. He ran in the neighborhood, and he ran with friends and family. His niece, Jimalee Humpton, tells her experience with running with her Uncle Dave:

> It was around 1972, and Uncle Dave and family were visiting ours in Unity, Maryland. It was a warm, pleasant spring morning. Uncle Dave laced up his jogging shoes and asked if I, his sixteen-year-old niece, would like to join him on a little run. I happily accepted his invitation, thinking I'd humor him and dampen my pace for this "old" guy. Surely, it would be an easy, abbreviated journey on the country road. Not so! Uncle Dave

comfortably led the way, far beyond the limits of my familiar little trek, conversing easily the whole time. (I was busy just trying to breathe!) Among other things, he communicated to me the pleasure of regular, lifelong exercise. Though I did not realize it that spring day in Maryland so long ago, but now that I look back, he surely deserves at least some of the credit for my ongoing love of long-distance running (including all its joys, friendships, opportunities, and health benefits) which continue to this very day. Thank you, Uncle Dave!

Dave kept records of his running. He would compete against himself in running more miles each year. His goal was to run more mileage than he would drive for vacation that year. So, he kept a chart to obtain his goal.

After Dave and I were married, we began a workout regimen. Dave, with his gift for organization, wrote out a workout plan, set goals, and kept a log of our activity and progress. He would modify the workout and change the sequence and number of repetitions. We worked out throughout our marriage using different machines, weights, biking and walking. We never ran together. Dave gave up running in 1989.

I put on my jogging shorts, laced up my shoes and started out the front door. I got part way down the street and it hit me. My wife, Iris, is lying upstairs in bed dying of cancer and here I am running to take care of my body. It's not right. I stopped, turned around and walked home.

Running had sustained him all his life, but at that moment, it was not right or fair. So, he stopped. He tried a few times later but lost the desire. In our marriage, we tried to stay physically active. Later on, Dave had hip replacements, back surgery, and knee replacement so running was no longer possible.

Dave did teach me to run in 2006. He taught me how to breathe while running, and how to begin with running and then walking and then increasing more running than walking. Then I began running every day. It was my way of dealing with the emotions, decline, and death of my mom. Now I run as my prayer time with my dog.

Dave always believed it was important to take care of your body, which is God's temple. He stayed active and physically fit throughout his life. He even asked the surgeon, after being diagnosed with brain tumors, if he could lift weights. The doctor looked at him, and said, "Are you serious?" Dave was serious. The doctor said, "No. Your body cannot take the strain." Dave continued to walk and move as long as possible.

Life Lesson

- Take care of your body. It is the temple of God. Get in shape. Stay in shape.

Physical Training

Dave was the PT (Physical Trainer) for the State Highway Patrol Academy within six months of graduating from the Academy himself. He later served as Commandant of the Training Academy. Several troopers who went through his training shared with Dave their memories:

"You were our PT instructor. The 56th academy class started the first week of February, 1961 at the old Hartman Farms. We did the PT outside and actually did pushups with snow up to our wrists. You would leave us in the front leaning rest position until we fell on our chest. You would then yell, 'All these truckers going down Route 23 see you on the ground and say to themselves, we can kick their rears.' This would bring us back up to the front leaning rest position. As the weather got better you would run us across country in recently tilled fields. We truly respected and loved you because everything you were making us do, you were also doing it and better. You taught us so much about getting in good physical condition."

—Ralph Lucas

"One of the jobs you gave me to do at the Academy was to take the bars from the Ohio State Pen riots and attach each end to a gallon can of cement to make barbells for weight lifting exercises."

—Jack Elsaesser

I received letters and stories from other retired troopers about their experiences with Dave as PT instructor:

"Mr. Sturtz informed us we were going to run around the entire circumference of the U.S. while in the academy. I thought, 'That's going to take a while.' Several cadets left that night. We ran a lot, but he was almost always with us."

—Ronald Teare

To truly understand who Dave was as PT instructor, I will let Tom Rice explain his first encounter with Dave and his training:

> I met David D. Sturtz on September 19, 1960 on a grassy field used for physical training in clear view of the old Hartman Farm building. A somewhat raspy but very strong voice in God-like tones, strong enough for workers in the vineyards to hear a half mile away announced, "My name is Dave Sturtz. I will be your PT Instructor."
>
> Everyone in the class knew immediately that a real man was in charge. We were about to enter on a physical journey we would never forget! During the next eight weeks for three hours per day, we were pushed to the point of exhaustion. However, Patrolman D.D. Sturtz did not demand we do anything that he did not do or could not do himself. He was always there in front of our class leading, guiding, directing and encouraging. He was encouraging us to do more and be more than we ever thought we could. Dave was working to build our mental toughness, to believe in ourselves, to be in the best physical condition that would allow us to breath and fight for ourselves or others when required.
>
> We often thought Dave stayed up nights thinking of ways to make us stronger. He brought in four by eight-inch construction bricks for us to run with and do push-ups on. Some of the bricks had holes through the center, and it would be a race by the class members before each PT session to get a set of these bricks. They were easier to hold with your fingers through the holes. Holding them was very important because it cost you twenty-five push-ups if you dropped a brick.

About two weeks into our physical training program, Dave drove past a gas station and noticed a display of tires wrapped in gold paper. The station manager told Dave those were old tires wrapped in gold paper to draw attention to a tire sale. The manager told Dave that when the sale was over he could have the tires. He made the trips back and forth hauling thirty-four tires in the trunk of his patrol car. When we saw the tires, we assumed it would be a simple exercise of running through the tires like we did in high school football practice. Wrong! We were marched into the center of an individual tire and brought to a halt. This tire would be our running mate for the next several weeks. We picked the tires up and held them around our waists and started our many journeys around the "grinder"—a gravel road around the three-acre exercise field. If that wasn't enough fun, we had games such as leapfrog and duck walking. There is nothing like thirty-four very tired men trying to jump over you all the while pushing you down into the gravel. We also had to climb a twenty-five-foot rope which was attached to a metal bar at the top of two old telephone poles. All of this hard work was to prepare us for boxing week and to get us into the best physical condition of our lives.

Dave enjoyed being the PT Instructor, and yes, he stayed awake at nights being innovative in creating ways to train. He had to build the training strategy along with the equipment. His goal was to get the cadets into their best physical condition so they could protect themselves and others in any situation as a Trooper.

Life Lesson

- Be in the best physical condition to do your job.

Obstacle Course

Dave maintained personal physical fitness throughout his Highway Patrol career. As a PT instructor, he prepared cadets to be in the best physical shape possible to do their jobs. When he became a District Commander, he took on the responsibility of training those in his command to be in the best shape physically and mentally to perform at the top level as a Trooper.

When Dave was promoted to Captain in the State Highway Patrol, he was assigned to the Findlay District Headquarters as the Commander. In the previous weeks on the patrol, Dave had traveled around the state, training the troopers for riot preparations. In this training, his assessment of District 1 (Findlay District) was *"the worst pit."* In Dave's own words, this is what happened:

> I was promoted to Captain and sent to District 1 as the Commander. The morale was punko. The leaders were good men, but they didn't know what to do. There was a DX (Driver License Examiner) assigned there, DX Palmerton, and his wife was my secretary. They owned a farm. He asked me if I liked honey and said to come by the farm. He lived beside the Blanchard River. So, one day I went out and saw the farm. I asked, "Would you loan me part of your property?"
>
> "What for?" he asked.
>
> "I'm going to build an obstacle course. I'm going to train the troops."
>
> He was a handyman so he cut logs. I put up ropes, sticks in trees for steps, and a rope across the river.

Once you started across, you had to keep going. It was the river or the stumps.

I ordered troopers from each post in the District to attend. I mixed them up. They had to climb an eight-foot wall and on the other side I had three-foot stumps they had to carry back to the beginning. I walked them through it.

We had rangers on the Patrol at that time. I had rangers there. Nobody from the District wanted to be there, and they were grumbling. I brought them back to the beginning. I told the troopers, "I've given the rangers a direct order. If any one of you slacks, stumbles or pretends not to know how to do this, I give these rangers permission to kick the hell out of you. You either run this course or I'll take care of you."

Now it's a different story. It's November, and we have snow, ice, and mud, too. But we are doing this. They jump, leap, fall. Trooper Brown broke his ankle. You'd have thought I committed murder. And then Reporter Shepherd from The Toledo Blade came out. He heard about it and the brutality of it. I said, "You can write a story if you run the course. If you don't run the course, you get no story. I'll run it with you." He ran it and ran a story. Well, by the third group of troopers, they were chanting and counting cadence.

Somebody out of the District complained to General Headquarters and Major Manly showed up. "What the hell you doing?" he yelled.

"This is an assignment. I ordered them to."

He took this back to the Colonel. I knew the Colonel wasn't going to say anything. I was doing my job.

115

> By the end of three months when District 1 went to the Academy for in-service training, they were saying, "We are from District 1, and we have an obstacle course. What do you do?" Pride. Accomplishment. Team.
>
> If you ran it once, I ran it with every group. I didn't have mercy or feel sorry for anyone. It was give a command and follow through. Promotions started to come out of a District where there had not been any. Leadership was sparked. The obstacle course did the job.

Dave had such a creative way of developing physical fitness. He used whatever was available. He was before his time in cross training. He saw the importance of being in the best shape possible to protect and serve.

> *"So let us run the race that is before us and never give up.*
> *We should remove from our lives anything*
> *that would get in the way*
> *and the sin that so easily holds us back."*
> *(Hebrews 12:1, NCV)*

Obstacles are part of our lives. We can face them and work through them, or we can sit on the sidelines and have self-pity and never accomplish anything. Dave used an obstacle course to teach troopers not just about physical fitness but about working together and overcoming the mental obstacles of life. He wanted them to take pride in who they were and what they could accomplish.

Life Lesson

- Face the obstacles of your life. You may get really muddy. It will be worth it. Learn and become better and stronger.

CHAPTER 8

INFLUENCE IN LIFE

Foundation of Influence

Dave credits his parents as the greatest influence in his life. They built the foundation of who he was and instilled in him the basics of honesty, integrity, respect, faith and family. Dave built his life on this firm foundation. He was influenced by his brothers, especially his older brother, Don, in his faith. Dave respected his elders and saw his teachers and coaches as role models for his life. He was influenced by one particular teacher.

> My favorite teacher whom I admired was Mrs. McGuire. She was my eighth-grade math teacher. She was firm but fair. She always called me "David." She had expectations not only of me but of everyone she taught. I did not want to disappoint her. I think sometimes I was afraid of her because I was unsure of myself at the time. One day after class, Mrs. McGuire stopped me by placing her hand on my shoulder. Instead of "getting a talking to," she told me never to change. "Be who you are and whatever you do, you will be successful because you are a good person." She didn't say I was a good boy or a good youth, but she referred to me as a person. I wanted to live up to her words.

The words of a teacher made an impact in Dave's life. It gave him confidence and a belief that he was important. Mrs. McGuire became part of Dave's extended family when his oldest brother, Don, married her step-daughter, Alice. Dave found out later in life that he was one of her favorite students, but she did not openly display this in the classroom. Her words of encouragement that one day spoke volumes into the life of an eighth-grade student.

"Be an example to the believers with your words,
your actions, your love, your faith and your pure life."
(1 Timothy 4:12, NCV)

Dave followed the example of his parents, his brothers, his teachers and coaches. He built his life on this foundation and became an example for others to follow. This is the cycle of life. You are influenced and guided by those who come before you. You are responsible to guide, instruct and be an example for those who follow after you.

Life Lesson

- Choose wisely whom you follow. Be aware that others are following you.

Influence on Youth

"You are God's children who he loves, so try to be like him."
(Ephesians 5:1, NCV)

Dave and I taught youth Sunday School class for years and were involved in the life of the youth while I was a Youth Minister. Dave used to say, "No youth wants to be around an old man. What do I have to offer them?" Dave offered life experiences to the youth. I taught the scriptures, and Dave told the stories. I would pause in my teaching, and Dave would begin "now here's a life lesson" and the stories would begin. The youth began to look forward to Dave's stories with life lessons.

"Dave leaned back in his chair. He had a story for everything but would always listen too. He never told you the answer but rather a story that helped you navigate."

—Mara Hughes

Dave made an impact in the lives of so many youths over the years. I share with you a few of their comments and stories in letters to Dave before his death.

"Thank you for sharing the love of Christ with me and my friends so many years ago."

—Trevor Miller

"What a difference you have made in my life. Your Sunday School talks and friendship were much appreciated. You have helped me get to where I am."

—Ryan Eich

"Your words of wisdom, knowledge and love are sure to guide us closer and closer to Jesus as we walk through life. You are truly an inspiration to me, and my love and respect grows more and more for you each day. If I didn't have a grandfather in my life, and I would most definitely want you to be that person."

—Scott Walsh

"Growing up in the church, I was blessed with many wonderful role models and teachers, but none of them influenced and guided me more than you. You taught me that it is important to ask yourself the tough questions: to establish where your values lie, and that faith is a living thing. You taught me that discussion, critical thinking, and daring to tackle the controversial aspects instead of avoiding them gives your faith the oxygen it needs to evolve, survive and grow. Before your class, I did not really grasp that faith is deeply personal, that faith is not black and white, the same as your parents or your peers; it is yours alone. As an adult now, this knowledge has allowed my relationship with God to grow in ways that wouldn't have been possible otherwise. Through yours and Elaine's Sunday School class, I also learned respect. As a teenager, respect is often eluded: both the giving and receiving sides. I was able to witness firsthand what genuine respect looks like. I learned that everyone's thoughts are valid, that you can respect and be respected even if you don't agree or think the same as someone else. You and Elaine always gave everyone a chance to express themselves, never passed judgment, and demanded the same for everyone else as well. By doing this, you were true disciples of Jesus—showing unconditional acceptance. I thank you, Dave, from the bottom of my heart for being a positive role model and helping me establish my 'Faith & Values.'"

—Cassie Harmon

And in letters and cards after Dave's death, former youth shared how Dave influenced their lives:

"We are better Christians and better people because Dave always encouraged us to be the best."

—Julie Daubenmire

"Dave always spoke his mind and encouraged me to do the same. He was always thoughtful and respectful."

—Emily Jennings

"I will always remember attending ninth grade Sunday School and Dave asking the class what our goals were for the future. I responded that I wanted to be a member of the Ohio State Marching Band. Each year through high school, Dave would make sure to confirm this was still my goal and asked what I had done recently to make progress toward this goal. After a few years of this, I began to feel a great sense of responsibility to make sure I was progressing towards my goals and dreams. What at first may have seemed like 'reporting back' my progress quickly turned into self-accountability for my actions. I always had Dave's voice in my head to drive me forward when times were tough. He not only took the time to ask meaningful and thoughtful questions, but he also made sure to follow up and offer encouragement. His teaching of setting goals, self-accountability, and offering encouragement no doubt contributed to me being a four-year member of the Ohio State Marching Band!"

—Andy Daubenmire

"I was honored that Dave was able to attend our wedding during the last months of his life. He left me with a great piece of marriage advice—'Just be nice to each other.' My life and faith is forever changed. He was a man who accomplished more than most of us can ever imagine and embodied everything a man of God should be."

—Caitlin Hughes Wood

"There are so many good memories I have of "Davey-Dale." He gave me drills to work on so I could be a better basketball player. He explained the many ways of killing a person with your bare hands… in Sunday School. And my favorite story of having a doorknob thrown at him while in the Highway Patrol. Most of all, I will remember his laugh and his big bear hugs."

—Ashley Ricket

"I remember my parents bringing home prescriptions for Dave and Elaine, and my Dad would always ask if I wanted to go with him to deliver them. Was that even a question? Going to Dave and Elaine's was like going to Disney. I loved it. Dave's stories were the best. I remember when Dave and Elaine came to a lacrosse game of mine, and I played terribly. Dave would always give the best advice. He told me to work hard and want it more than anyone else. Mostly, I remember his hugs—like a big, gentle bear!"

—Abby Ricket

Dave also taught several youths how to drive.

"Dave was a very special man. Not only was he the man who taught me how to drive, but he was my friend. Before each driving lesson we would start with prayer. During my driving lessons he instilled confidence in me I didn't know I had. I was very blessed to call Dave my friend."

—Rachel Lyle

Many of the former youth who now have families of their own came to the visitation and celebration of Dave's life to show respect to a man who treated them as valuable persons. He listened to them, he told them stories, and he loved them and was part of their foundation of faith. Dave made a difference in the lives of countless youth who are living their faith because of Dave's willingness to be a part of their lives as the *"old man"* and share lessons for life through the stories of his own life.

Life Lesson

• Invest yourself in the youth. Pour your love, care and life lessons into them.

Influence on Adults

Youth were not the only ones influenced by Dave and his life lessons and stories. Here are a few adults sharing Dave's influence in their lives.

> "So, what was it about Dave? His personality was infectious from his laugh to his stories. He was a rock I could always lean on. He listened and would offer his words of wisdom. His moral compass was always pointed to the true North. He always told me he would have been a mountain man if it were another time and place. I think he was, just in a patrol cruiser. Good or bad everyone has a story and Dave would listen. Work harder, be smarter, always do your best, that was Dave. He made you want to be a better person. And as Dave always said, 'aim low, they may be riding short ponies.' Expect the unexpected; that's life, that's Dave."
>
> —Jim *Ricket*

> "Dave had a way of making you feel as though you were the only one there! It warmed our hearts how he would ask how 'our Ben' (grandson) was.

Dave was such an honorable and awesome role model. It has been our great honor and privilege to call him friend."

—LeeAnne & Jeff Davis

"I loved when he was getting ready to tell you something. There was this depth of thought first. He had your full attention as you knew you wanted to hear what he had to say. His message didn't mince nor waste words. But the moment I loved was the slight twinkle or grin. Not always sure if he said all he was thinking, but he knew and understood the moment."

—Shirley Kruse

"There are many people who come and go in our lives, but few have touched us the way you and Dave have done. We are better for knowing you both. We will be forever grateful for Dave's kindness. He was a man of great integrity, compassion and honesty."

—Don & Ginny Schlosser

"How fortunate our teenagers were to experience Dave's guidance and Christian example through Sunday School and youth activities. Our Stephen Ministry classes were filled with his real-life stories and scenarios to learn from. As a staff member, I (Jenny) benefited from his fair, honest, down to earth methods of administration. Through these and many other memories, Dave lives on."

—Mike & Jenny Miller

"I will always appreciate the time and love you poured into my sons as well as Tom and myself. We have all grown and learned from you and been blessed."

—Sandy Kincaid

"The Sunday School class you taught years ago; how much that class and your Christian witness helped us to grow in our spiritual life."

—Linda & Roger Scheetz

"When Roger and I first met Dave, we found out that he had a daughter named Gretchen and so from that moment on it seemed a special bond formed. In all the years I knew Dave, he never failed to give me a hug and a kiss on the cheek. Dave was a blessing in so many ways to me and there are no words to express the special bond we shared. He was more than a friend, and I loved him very much. I miss his special smile, I miss his wonderful laugh, and I especially miss his hug and kiss on the cheek."

—Gretchen Solt

"David worked with older people (when he volunteered with hospice). I asked him one time what he believed older people living alone missed the most. I was expecting to hear the loss of youth, sight, hearing or mobility. Without the least moment of thought, David said, 'Another human's touch.' The simplicity of it was profound. I've practiced doing that every time since, when appropriate."

—Don VanMeter

"I always admired Dave's strength, strong character, values and a sense of humor that always seemed to place things in proper perspective. I learned from Dave that his strength came from his faith in God. He told me it is how you react that determines how others feel. Dave was a strong man and I gained wisdom and strength from his words. He continued to place others before self his entire life."

—Scott Lorenzo

"The impact he had upon me was truly life changing. His influence was like a bomb blast that sent me forward, propelling me to become a confident, strong woman who is fearless. He was such an amazing person who believed in me when I questioned myself. I look back on the achievements in my life and know that he was the reason I was able to do the things that once seemed impossible. Years later, I was lucky enough to have the opportunity to thank him and tell him how grateful I was for his friendship and support and how much it changed my life. He was my mentor, my friend, and a second dad. I would have never let him down or disappointed him. I am sure I'm one of many who look back on the transforming affect he had upon our lives. I will always be grateful to have had the chance for Dave Sturtz to grace my life."

—Janet Journey

And from one of his friends on the Highway Patrol and former Director of the Secret Service, John describes Dave and his influence:

"Many times when one hears so many positive comments and stories about an individual, there is a disappointment or let down upon meeting and knowing them. Not so with David. He impressed me until his death. He truly loved God. Oh, boy, wow, when David stepped into a classroom, onto an athletic field or out of his Highway Patrol vehicle, the picture was impressive, attractive, strong, authoritative, friendly, business-like but fair and constructive. He was a man of God, yet a man's man, solid as a rock inside and out with the smile of an excited teenager and compassion for all people. When he stands before a Highway Patrol class of recruits or new supervisors, there is total attention and respect. He is a guy who has been there and his demeanor is captivating."

—John Magaw

When Dave was the Assistant Safety Director for the City of Columbus, he worked on a Police investigation with Police Commander Jim Dean. Here is Jim's impression of Dave:

"Dave was very open and sharing in who and what he was about. He was also very humble for someone who had achieved so much and had gone so far, and yet his real loyalty was to God and his family and friends. I was honored then and still today and always will be to be included as a friend of his. Dave seemed to have the greatest respect of everyone where we went. We visited many OSP and other State offices. Whoever was there stood up to shake his hand and referred to him as 'The Major' or 'Inspector General'."

—Jim Dean

Highway Patrol Influence

When Dave was first diagnosed with brain tumors, an email went out to the State Highway Patrol retirees about his condition. Included in that message was an opportunity for retirees to write to Dave and let him know what difference he made in their lives and to share stories with him. Here are a few excerpts from those letters:

"Throughout my career, I have looked up to and admired you as a man of integrity who was not afraid to tell the truth. Not only did you set the example for me; you were the example! You are a true professional in every sense of the word."

—Gil Jones

"I remember so well one of your comments when we were confronted with a prison riot. You said, 'Give me a couple troops and we will surround them and defeat them.' You were always positive and had a terrific impact on the Patrol in such a positive manner."

—Ed Suffecool

"You had an enormous influence on me. I clearly remember the uplifting speeches of in-service training that would send all of us home thinking we could lick the world. You always inspired a small but effective force to follow your lead. You always made us believe we could accomplish the impossible…and we often did."

—Tim Del Vecchio

"You had a tremendous leadership ability and after the riot training, I was convinced I would follow you through the gates of hell if there was someone inside we had to arrest. We have been through parts of heaven and hell together and in your words, 'have some scar tissue on us', but it has made us both better people. I just wanted you to know how much you have affected my life and how much I have always admired and respected you."

—Bob Welsh

"You are a devout Christian whom I have always held in the highest esteem and looked up to as a role model for my life and for my OSHP career. You have never failed me. You will always be one of the most respected men I have ever known."

—Don Slemmer

"You have been a major inspiration throughout my life. Honesty, dedication, truthfulness, and fairness are the words that come to mind when I think of you and the impact you had on me throughout my life."

—Ron Hoeft

"Your character and professionalism had a profound positive affect on me and my career. I am a better person for having had the privilege of knowing and working with you."

—Ed Farris

"You have always been the consummate leader and motivator. It was the way you addressed us and the exemplary example you provided to everyone of what a real Ohio State Highway Patrolman was. Both of those were certainly part of what made you the leader you were and are, but there has always been that extra quality about you that made us not want to ever disappoint you. I have very few heroes who had a dramatic influence on my success in and enjoyment of my service in the OSHP. You have been and remain one of those few. Thank you for who you are, for everything you have always stood for, for all you did for Ohio State Patrol and for allowing me to know you and learn from you."

—Mike Quinn

"I was impressed with your charismatic leadership, outstanding public speaking skills and overall 'command' presence. Throughout my career, I have always tried to emulate and live up to the ethical and leadership standards that you set for yourself and demanded in others."

—Bill Healy

"The more time I spent with you, the more I came to appreciate your wisdom and guidance. One of the most impressive things about you was that I truly felt you cared about me as a young trooper and a person. You expressed interest in my thoughts and motivations. You listened. I developed a very healthy respect for your knowledge, wisdom and compassion."

—Lance Mathess

"Your words to me were – 'Do something! Even you might get it right.' The flavor of my many failures was softened because I knew and you knew I tried."

—R.A. Smith

R.A. Smith and his wife, Jonnie Sue, wrote Dave a letter every two weeks throughout his illness. Dave loved the "down home" adventures that he shared. R.A. got it right and brought a smile to Dave in those letters.

Many of the stories of Dave's Highway Patrol career were told in a previous chapter. This chapter shares words from those who were influenced by Dave. These words describe the difference Dave made in the lives of former Highway Patrol Troopers and the impact Dave's life had on their lives:

"Walt joined the patrol in 1965 and was thrilled when he made it through the academy. He was assigned to the Ashtabula Post and paired with a trooper who was to be his Coach. Unfortunately, their personalities did not mesh at all, and it wasn't long before Walt's enthusiasm wore off and his desire to be a trooper was no longer there. A young Corporal by the name of D.D. Sturtz arrived at the post and assessed the situation. He took Walt under his wing, and from that day on he was a totally different person. If it had not been for Dave, Walt would not have stayed, that would have been such a tragedy because Walt absolutely loved his job. Dave made an impact on Walt's life and career."

—Pat Ashbridge (wife)

I share two stories from Gary Smith. Dave always said that he would have adopted Gary as his second son. Dave had a gift of perception. He could look within a person and see the potential and the special qualities and find ways of developing those qualities to bear fruit.

"Major Dave was the man solely responsible for allowing me to enter the OSHP Academy in 1974. I was having trouble passing the 'color-vision' eye tests, but after providing Major Dave with five letters of support from various optometrists, Major Dave, with permission from Col. Chiaramonte and Major Gilmartin, told me he would allow me to enter the 99th class. It was on one condition, that if I ever did anything wrong, or screwed up in any way, he would personally fire me. He said this with a sly grin on his face and a sparkle in his eye. He literally saved my life that day by giving me the nod to enter the OSP Academy."

—Gary Smith

"A few months later, October 9, 1974 to be exact, the Wednesday morning I was to start the Academy, my mom died in her sleep, and I almost did not attend the Academy. Major Dave told me and Dad to report and check in. I did, and then he allowed me as many days necessary to be away for the funeral. He even took the time to personally attend my mom's funeral. This great man showed me what love and family really meant. I will love him forever."

—Gary Smith

"Dave taught me a very valuable lesson that regardless of your rank or importance in life, it is always a tremendous gesture to take the time to acknowledge the accomplishments of those around you. This is a trait taught to me by one of the most respected individuals I have ever been associated with, not only in my career with the Patrol, but in life. It is a tradition that I still carry forward today with those around me."

—Bob Markowski

"Dave was probably one of the most intense, focused individuals I have ever met. He was a man who seemed to speak more with his actions than his words. I wanted to be like him. He was such a strong individual."

—Gerald (Jerry) Sewell

"Dave Sturtz was simply one tough cookie that no one messed with. He was a naturally genuine gentleman with a very bright and optimistic outlook on life. The other admirable attribute, not generally associated with a disciplinarian, was his terrific sense of humor. Many tense situations were made bearable following one of his discreetly placed 'humorisms' followed by a smile or appropriate chuckle. To better describe my feelings about Dave as a leader and a friend, if he asked me if I would accompany him to Mars but that it would have to be done by bicycle, I'd ask when we were leaving."

—Ed Waltz

"David has left his mark on this earth. He was a wonderful person, a leader, listener, and full of love, compassion, and many talents but, above all, he shared being a Christian with everyone. He will be missed, but not forgotten. He was my friend and I thank God for his friendship."

—Don Anweiler

"Dave's influence has inspired many, including me, to do their best in all endeavors. I hold Dave in the highest esteem."

—Gene Archer

"I always loved Dave's personal attitude. If he was ever down, he did not show it. I am a very fortunate man to have counted Dave Sturtz as my personal friend. His integrity, honesty and plain speaking while addressing people directly, looking them in the eye, was a quality Dave had that not many people have."

—Dave Furiate

The last two gentlemen, Rob Hartsell and Tom Rice, were special friends to Dave. They shared years together in their work careers from Highway Patrol, Consultants, Safety Directors and Homeland Security. Their stories have been included in the Highway Patrol Chapter and they have assisted with many of the stories.

> "We all learned life lessons from Dave Sturtz. He taught us many things without ever saying a word. He taught by example and his mere presence, countenance and demeanor. What did we learn? We learned to believe in ourselves and to never give up. We learned that we could do more than we ever thought we could. We learned from Dave that when things were difficult for others, it was just right for us. We learned respect for hard work, doing the job completely and how we should treat everyone with dignity and respect regardless of their station in life. We all learned that life is not fair, and it is not what happens to you but how you react to what happens to you that builds character. Finally, we learned about Dave's sense of humor. No one could tell stories the way Dave told stories. Dave's qualities, character and integrity had a tremendously positive influence on the Ohio State Patrol and hundreds of thousands who had the good fortune to know him."
>
> —Col. Tom Rice (retired)

"Dave's positive personality, appearance and leadership abilities were qualities that he exhibited the first time I met him and throughout his career. I strived to emulate him. He set the example of the 'right way' and I learned much from him. Over my career, I was often faced with difficult situations where an action or decision was called for and I thought, 'What would Dave do?' He never had to 'blow his own horn' or 'try to impress others.' He just set the example of a professional in all that he did and inspired others. People respected him and followed his lead. I know I did! The thing that I appreciated and learned the most from Dave was how he lived his faith in God. He didn't flaunt it, he didn't preach it, but he just lived it and set the example for others to follow. The faith journey is a tough one, especially for someone who is in a semi-military setting, strong physically and mentally, and has strong natural leadership abilities. But his faith was always evident in everything he did without his pointing it out. Everyone just knew he cared about others and was a man of God because of his actions and treatment of others. I'm sure many learned from him how to be a Christian in such an environment. I know I did."

—Rob Hartsell

Many more people could share in this chapter. I have just taken excerpts from some of the cards and letters I have received. The purpose of sharing the influence Dave had on the lives of others is not to say Dave was perfect or better than others. It is to share that Dave built his life on the foundation of his faith, values and principles. He was grounded in his faith in God. He loved God, and he loved people. Dave used his God-given strengths of leadership and his personality to bring out the best in others. His stories influenced people, but who he was as a person connected him to others. Dave's life made a difference.

"The Lord is pleased with those who respect him,
with those who trust his love."
(Psalm 147:11, NCV)

Life Lesson

- We are all called to make a difference in this world, to influence the lives of others for good and for God. What is the legacy you are leaving for others to follow? What will people say about you?

CHAPTER 9

FRIENDS AND FAMILY RELATIONSHIPS

Friendship

"Some friends may ruin you,
but a real friend will be more loyal than a brother."
(Proverbs 18:24, NCV)

"A friend loves you all the time,
and a brother helps in time of trouble."
(Proverbs 17:17, NCV)

This is Dave's description of the friends in his life: "I have had good friends who loved me, stood by me, and put up with me, and I have done the same with them, unconditionally. All have shared happy times with me and sad times with me, but all of it has been shared with the feelings of the heart and mind. They have been there and have been true and loyal and loving friends."

To have friends, you have to be a friend and have the qualities of a friend. In a true and abiding friendship, you know who you are, have goals and directions for your own life, and you share these with those who love and support you.

This is Dave's description of how he wanted to be remembered:

> I would like to be remembered by my friends as an honest person who told the truth, stood by my principles—sometimes stubbornly, but people would know where I stood on issues and in difficult times. I want to be remembered as a person who upheld the Sturtz name and was loyal.

Life Lesson

- Be a friend.

Childhood Friendships

I had two best friends in school, Gary Cosmar and Herb Chilcote. Herb and I went to school together from first grade through graduation. Gary became part of our friendship in seventh grade. From seventh grade until graduation we were inseparable. We played sports together, ate at each other's houses and each of our moms took a special liking to the others.

As Jr. High boys, the three had quite the adventures running the streets of Coshocton in the summers. One of the stories Dave tells is about his stealing a watermelon with his friends:

An old man grew watermelons down by the river. He had a huge patch, and in the summer, kids would steal from his patch. He kept an eye on the melons. One day we were near the area, and we were hot and hungry. 'Let's get a watermelon and see who can swim the fastest across the river with the melon.' I'm not sure who decided it would be a great idea, but we all grabbed one. So, I grabbed a watermelon and jumped into the river with the melon and then I heard the shots. The old guy had a pellet gun and was shooting rock salt at us. The others let go of the melons but I held on to mine and bam! I was hit in the side. I kept swimming and made it to the other side of the river. I was bleeding from being shot. We went to Coz's house and poured peroxide on it and it burned. We wrapped it and I never told my mom. Every day for a couple of weeks, my friends would help me clean it and wrap it.

Dave never told his mom about it until years later. He had the scars from being shot with rock salt all of his life.

Herb Chilcote shares these words about his friendship with Dave:

> Dave and I met in first grade at South Lawn School and became friends in that year. We became best friends through high school. Dave and I participated in football and basketball. I was Captain of the football team, and Dave was Captain of the basketball team. I think we were together almost daily. When we entered junior high school, we met a new student named Gary Cosmar. He became our friend, and we were sometimes referred to as 'The Three Musketeers.' Those days were some of the best of my life.

The friendship of Gary Cosmar and Dave was a lifelong friendship. Even though they went their separate ways after graduation, they kept in touch throughout their lives. Gary or "Coz" as he was called was always dressed in the latest style while Dave was a jeans and t-shirt guy. Gary's mom, *"Mother Mary"* as Dave called her, treated Dave like a second son. Over the years, Dave and Coz visited with one another, and Mother Mary was a part of the visit.

The one word that describes Dave and his friendships is loyalty. Dave was a loyal friend. He stayed true to a friend through the good and the struggles of life. One day, Dave received a call from Coz with the news that he had a brain tumor. Dave was on a plane to Florida to be with his friend. They shared a wonderful visit that included an Orlando Magic basketball game and hours of stories and memories. Then a few months later, the call came that Coz was in a coma. We were on a plane and Dave sat at bedside with Coz for nine days until death.

Dave said,

> Coz was the loyal friend. It didn't matter where he moved or I moved, he made sure we stayed connected. We were best friends and that is what friends do for one another. I wouldn't have been anywhere else but with him until the end.

I had the privilege of officiating at Gary's memorial service. Dave had the privilege of saying good-bye to his lifelong friend and to be with "Mother Mary" in her grief. Dave continued to be the second son throughout "Mother Mary's" life. He kept in touch, and we were part of her memorial service too.

Life Lesson

- A friend is with you in the joys of life and doesn't leave you when life gets tough and sad.

Friendships

Dave had life-long friendships from his years on the highway patrol. Tom Rice and Rob Hartsell shared in the previous chapters about Dave's influence and his stories. In the eulogy they shared at Dave's funeral, Tom and Rob ended their talk by sharing words that described their best friend and brother:

> "Honest, loyal, truthful, ethical, friendly to all, always did his best, he loved his family and was a decisive leader."

> —Tom

"Compassionate, respectful, caring – cared for others, encouraging, love of people, made others feel good, people liked to be around Dave, role model, and a hugger."

—Rob

Many people considered Dave their friend. He was a friend who lived out the words that Tom and Rob used to describe him. Two men that Dave talked about all the time as dear friends who made a difference in his life and helped him to be the best trooper possible were Chet Hayth and Merle Darrah.

Dave described Merle as *"one of the smartest men on the Highway Patrol."* Merle was Dave's coach after he graduated from the Academy and went to his first assignment at the Lisbon Patrol Post. Dave rode with Merle for two weeks and then Merle set him free. Merle was always available to guide and assist, but Dave was given the freedom to develop and set his own path. A bond of respect formed with this type of guidance and leadership. Both Dave and Merle had deep respect for one another and the gifts they each had enhanced their friendship. Dave said of Merle,

> He always taught with examples. He would use "what if" —"what if something took place, what would you do?" He was always testing you. He was not afraid to tell you that you got it right and was not bashful telling you that you were wrong. He was a man of his word. He was a great storyteller and enjoyed running people through mind mazes. Merle was like my uncle. He taught me things I used throughout my career.

Dave and Chet Hayth met at the beginning of Dave's Patrol career and worked together throughout their career. Their lives together were filled with many stories. They were friends through difficult situations and events, but through it all they remained loyal and true to one another. They spent family time, vacations and holidays together. Their friendship represented a stand for what was right even if it jeopardized one's career. Dave said, "I learned how to do things from Chet the way they needed to be done."

The OSP friendships went deep and lasted through moves, retirements and new opportunities. The Patrol was family. Dave was the person who received the call in the night, and he would go to the aid of a friend.

> *"Greater love has no one than this,*
> *that he lay down his life for his friends."*
> *(John 15:13, NIV)*

Dave was this kind of friend, willing to lay down his life in support of a friend. He had your back and was loyal and trustworthy, and he expected the same in return. This is sacrificial love. Dave was never shy about saying *"I love you."* He would openly hug his friends, male and female. As a friend, Dave encouraged you to think for yourself. He challenged you to grow and was accountable to his friends.

Dave was in an Emmaus Share Group for years after attending the Walk to Emmaus Spiritual Weekend. Ray Belfrage was one of the friends in the share group for years. Ray said, "Dave was always prepared. He would bring something extra to the group each time to talk about and challenge us."

Dave and Roger Solt were share partners for several years. Roger describes their time together:

> Dave helped me to stay focused on God and family and keep my priorities in order. If I was having a tough week, he was encouraging to me. But most of all, Dave was an excellent listener. I always felt like he was very interested in whatever was going on in my life.

Dave had a genuine interest in the lives of others. He listened, wanting to know more about his friends and the struggles and concerns. Dave listened and was then able to share a perspective that gave understanding and insight.

Life Lesson

- True friendship is sacrificial and being willing to lay down your life for your friend.

Family

"I'm blessed when it comes to family." —Dave

Dave's first friends were his brothers. The Sturtz brothers share a special bond. They love each other, respect each other, are loyal and protective of one another, and support one another. They have similar traits instilled in them through their parents, but they are each unique and gifted in their own way. Dave loved their bond and their differences. Dave was the connector for his brothers.

His brother, Ken, describes Dave's life: "Dave remains as a true guidepost for living the good life."

There was and will always be a deep love and respect between the brothers.

Dave was also a beloved uncle. One of his nieces, Janel Hemmen, wrote about her uncle when she was in sixth grade many years ago. Janel reflects on those words:

> "Uncle Dave loved. A lot. He loved God. He loved his family. He loved his country. He loved his job. He loved telling stories. He loved to laugh. The following anecdote was written for a sixth grade English assignment in October of 1971, and I happened to come across it in time to read it to Uncle Dave one of the last times I saw him.
>
> > *"I have an uncle who is very funny and is quite a character. He is so funny and has such a great sense of humor that I think that he could make anyone laugh. His occupation is working as a Captain for the Ohio State Patrol. One time, when he was not in uniform, he entered a restaurant to have dinner. Some men sitting in the booth beside him noticed that he was sitting alone, and they asked him to join them. While my uncle drank his coffee with them, they had been drinking beer and they were now pretty well drunk. They had also been laughing and talking about driving home in this condition. After a while they got around to asking my uncle where he worked. When he replied, 'The State Patrol', they all laughed and hollered and stamped their feet, saying that this was the funniest joke they had ever heard!"*

Forty-five years later Uncle Dave was still laughing, and loving, and being loved. I loved my uncle dearly, not just because he was funny and had so many interesting stories to tell. He was what some might call a "gentle giant," strong, impressive, and commanding, yet gentle, kind, warm, and compassionate. He was a man of integrity, honor, and dignity, with strong convictions and unwavering beliefs and values.

Another niece, Jimalee Humpton, wrote these words to her Uncle Dave about a month before he died:

Uncle Dave, you have always served as such a positive influence in my life, in the formation of my values and in my faith in Jesus Christ. You are one of the important pieces in my happy, fun-filled childhood. I can recall your voice sharing amazing stories of your unique adventures serving on the Ohio State Patrol. Your trust in the Almighty God in the midst of heartache and loss has helped to build my faith.

Jimalee's husband, Lyle Humpton, describes Uncle Dave: "His love for life, his Lord and Savior Jesus Christ and his big manly hugs…and the kiss on the cheek! And lastly his words ….'I love you'."

Dave's Uncle Karl describes his nephew: "Dave was a tough-hearted Christian. You don't run into people like the Sturtz brothers. Dave was at the top of the list."

Dave's sister-in-law, Alice Sturtz, shares about her memories of Dave:

Dave became a part of my life when I was fourteen and Dave was ten. His older brother, Don, was my "boyfriend." Back then, Dave was a friendly little guy who was always eager to tell me about his latest homerun or a venture with his buddies on Vine Street. In school, Dave did well partly because there was not one teacher able to get mad at him including my step-mother, Laura McGuire, who taught eighth grade math. Dave was so genuine and would easily turn on the charm. My Aunt Mary, a spinster school teacher, visited often for our family occasions. Dave would always greet her with a hug which was not a common thing back then. Aunt Mary loved that and she came to expect a hug at every event from Dave. As Dave's sister-in-law, I will always remember him with a smile. His faith, strength, loyalty, honesty, wit, and love live on.

Family is about love and sharing life together. Dave loved life and loved the people in his life. Whoever he was with, he was all in and present. You had his attention and you gave him your full attention, not wanting to miss a story or a life lesson. What made the relationships so special was Dave's sense of humor, his stories, his laughter, but most importantly his love.

Life Lesson

* Love your family.

Children and Grandchildren

Each Christmas and birthday, Dave wrote a letter to his children and grandsons. The letter explained the gift he was giving them or described the love he had for them. Here is part of a letter he wrote to his daughter, Gretchen, for her birthday in 2008:

My Dearest Daughter Gretchen Ann,

I remember your birth like it was only yesterday. What a thrill and joy when the nurse came out and told me, "Your wife is just fine. You have a beautiful baby girl." Over the years there have been up and down times, but in my heart and eyes you have never changed. You are still my beautiful baby girl. Time and things change. You are a strong woman, and you have your best days yet in front of you. Each day I pray for your happiness and that your life will be filled with positive and rewarding love. Stay strong in your faith, take care of your son and know that you are loved by our entire family.

Love, Dad

Dave's daughter, Gretchen, shares a couple special memories about her Dad:

One of the stories that my Dad would tell about me included a red wagon. When he was stationed in Lancaster and worked the night shift, my Dad took care of me during the day while my Mom worked. He would take me on long walks while pulling me in my red wagon. He would pull his little red-haired daughter in her little red wagon for miles. He was a proud father whom I loved so very much.

In his story about our wagon walks, he said that I would raise my hand and wave and yell out "HELLO" to everyone we passed by. As I got older and would hear him tell this story, I thought he was just making fun of me as a three-year-old. I always loved every one of his stories, no matter how many times I had heard it.

I was visiting my Dad in the hospital when he was diagnosed with brain tumors and had a biopsy.

When it was time for him to get up and walk, I was given a harness to assist if needed. He held on to his IV pole, and we went out into the hospital hallway. I was worrying about making sure he did not fall while my dad was waving his hand to each and every person he passed, telling them "HELLO" and addressing something personal to each one, spreading his positivity and upbeat energy. That was my Dad. He shared himself with everyone. When we returned to the hospital room and he sat down, I thought about that little red-haired girl waving to everyone she saw and yelling out "HELLO!"

Yes, I am my father's daughter, and what a blessing to be given him as my Dad. In my heart, now that he has passed, I believe that my Dad's job in Heaven is the Welcome Ambassador, welcoming all the people and especially those that might be unsure or frightened. He had such a knack for pulling people in and making them feel safe. He always did that for me. I love you, Dad!

—Gretchen Sturtz

Dave loved being a Grandpa to his two grandsons, O'Shay and Chris. He tried to stay involved in their activities and enjoyed time with them in our home and on trips. Dave's legacy lives on through the impact he made in the lives of his two grandsons. I will let them share their stories. First, from O'Shay:

One of my favorite childhood memories are the sleep overs at Grandpa and Elaine's house with my cousin, Chris. We spent hours in the basement playing made up games using a little rubber soccer ball. During one heated match, the ball rolled into the dark scary part of the basement where Chris and I refused to go. Being the observant person Grandpa was, he used this information to make up one of his elaborate stories about the monster who lived in the back corner of their basement. Grandpa sat Chris and me down and made it abundantly clear to NOT go into that part of the basement because he could not protect us against the basement monster. He picked up the boot (the one we later found out was his that he wore for an injured foot) and said, 'I went down there two days ago and I wrestled, I fought, and barely escaped, but I escaped with the basement monster's shoe!' He proceeded to hold the boot high which obviously made two little boys scream and promise never to go on that side of the basement ever.

From the time I started playing sports at age five through my senior year in high school, my Grandpa came to all my sporting events. I do not remember him ever missing a game. He was never shy about expressing his feelings at the games toward the referees, the coaches and even toward me. After each game, I looked for my Grandpa and received the biggest hug and kiss on the cheek from him. Regardless of how I played, I knew my Grandpa was always proud of me and that meant more than winning or losing to me.

One of my favorite memories about my Grandpa was having lunch with him from the time I was in first grade until a few weeks before he passed. I valued these lunches because of the knowledge and perspective my Grandpa provided me on an array of topics. He was never bias toward me, and he was always 100% honest with me. His honesty was one of Grandpa's best traits. He would tell you how it is. He had the unique ability to do this while being 100% respectful. Those lunch time talks provided me with invaluable insight on how to deal with day to day problems. I still use the lessons I learned from those lunches in my everyday life.

My Grandpa Sturtz was the most honest, hardworking, stand up, do right, loving and caring person I have ever known. Not a day goes by that I don't wish I could spend one more day with him. I love you, Grandpa.

—O'Shay Mallory

Now, his grandson, Chris, shares about the influence his Grandpa Sturtz had and continues to have on his life:

David D. Sturtz is my Grandpa and the greatest man I have ever known. Growing up, I was very fortunate to spend time with my Grandpa and Elaine. We spent summers together and took trips with my cousin, O'Shay. I remember my Grandpa being a very strong and respected man. When I played sports and Grandpa helped coach, everyone worked harder and his presence brought the team together. He influenced the team to give 100% with a never quit attitude. Grandpa instilled in me the importance of God, honesty, hard work, and a very common theme in my everyday life, to always do what is right. My Grandpa has been and continues to be my greatest role model.

He was always pushing me to do my best. He made me want to be better every day just because I never wanted to disappoint him. Grandpa was there in the key moments of my life and always supportive. He was a great motivator. When I became a firefighter/paramedic, Grandpa was proud of me, but he still let me know his confidence in me was very high wanting me to pursue my potential.

As an adult, he watched me get married, begin my firefighter/paramedic career, and become a father. He became a Great Grandpa with the births of Brooklyn, Makenna and Addisyn. One of his favorite stories was telling the story of Addisyn's birth. Addisyn was born in our bathroom. She came so quickly that I delivered her before the ambulance arrived. I can still remember the smile on Grandpa's face as he would tell this story.

Since going home to Heaven, my Grandpa has continued to watch over and be part of my family. I can imagine his smile when our son, Caden David Sturtz, was born just a few months after his passing. Grandpa was excited to be the first person in the family to be told our fourth and last child was a boy and would be given 'David' as his middle name. I can still feel the hug and hear him say, "Good job Sturtz" when I won the Grand National Champion Award competing in the Fire Fighter Combat Challenge. He always took physical fitness very seriously especially for public safety workers. I know he is proud. I can feel the strong handshake from him when I was promoted. I share these accomplishments not to brag but to express the power of his positive influence. He has molded me in every aspect of my life and I owe him so much for it. I know he is still with me and I think of him often.

I learned from my Grandpa—"Always do what is right." This is how I live my life, every aspect of my life. It is simple yet not always easy to do. I challenge you to use that in your life as I do because of my Grandpa. His favorite Bible verse from Joshua 1:9, guides me in life as a father, husband and firefighter/paramedic. I know my Grandpa lived this verse. I have never known a better man than him or a stronger man of God. I know he is in Heaven watching over us, and I will see him again someday.

—Chris Sturtz

Life Lesson

- Make a positive difference in the lives of your children and grandchildren. Leave a legacy.

CHAPTER 10

STRUGGLES OF LIFE

"He Is My Son"

Over the years of conversations with Dave, the one struggle he continued to try and figure out and have regrets about was with his son, Craig. Dave loved being a father to his daughter, Gretchen, and his son, Craig. Over a ten-year period of time, Dave said his career was his focus. He went wherever he was sent, stayed as long as he was needed, and gave everything within him to solve the problem. He was gone from home for long periods of time during the formative years of his children. He was present for ball games and family events, but in day-to-day living, he was gone.

Dave would say, "I feel like I have failed as a parent." He took on the issues and problems with his son as his own. Craig lived in addiction for almost thirty years. This chapter is not a focus on Craig and the addictions. It is not to glorify evil. This period of time for Dave was filled with lies, hurts, stealing, visits to his son in prison, broken promises, forgiveness, and a hope that someday the hold of addiction would be broken.

Dave told his brothers in their last visit together:

> I brought my son into this world and as a father I needed to stick by him. I never stopped loving him. He's my son. I didn't love what he did, but I always loved him. I never gave up on him.

Dave never knew how to help his son. He was angry, frustrated, hurt and disappointed. He would yell and scream and try to set boundaries and show tough love.

But Dave would want to believe his son so much that he would believe the lies, thus enabling the addiction.

Dave would ask, "I can help other people, even strangers and influence them for good, why can't I help my son?"

Dave would have given and did give anything to help his son. Dave prayed for his son. He gave financially. When he began to realize that he could not help his son and that financial support was not helping, he turned to me one day and said, "Addiction is like pouring money down a rat hole."

Dave knew he could not fix this even though he wanted to find a way to fix his son. Craig had to be the one to seek help. Oh, they had been through every addiction treatment center in the area. They were never enough. Craig had to finally surrender. Dave had to surrender, too, that he could not help or heal his son. Only God could, which was one of the hardest lessons for Dave to learn.

Craig finally surrendered to Jesus and allowed God to be the center of his life, not the demons of addiction. Craig became a new creation.

> *"Therefore, if anyone is in Christ, he is a new creation;*
> *the old has passed away, behold, the new has come."*
> *(2 Corinthians 5:17, RSV)*

Dave received the gift he had prayed for in the last two years of his life. His son, Craig, was a new creation through Jesus Christ. The demons of addiction were gone. He was clean and sober, but most importantly he was and is Christ-centered and Spirit-filled. The gift was given and received with open arms. Dave was able to hug his son in the last months of Dave's life knowing Craig was a new creation in Jesus.

Life Lesson

• Surrendering to God is a hard lesson to learn, but once we do, God takes the demons of our lives and brings healing and hope. We cannot fix other people's lives. Give them to God. God is the great Healer.

Disappointment

Once Dave became a member of the Ohio State Highway Patrol and began to be promoted through the ranks, he set his career goal to become the Superintendent of the State Highway Patrol. He was the youngest promoted through the ranks to Major. It seemed like the natural next step for one who was respected and admired within the ranks.

Dave's greatest career disappointment was not being named the Superintendent of the State Highway Patrol. Not having his friend and fellow trooper, Chet Hayth, named as Superintendent was his second greatest disappointment.

Ginny Fogt was a trooper assigned to Headquarters during this time:

> When I was assigned to the Inspections and Standards, I shared an office space with Major Sturtz. Major Sturtz was what you might call a "black sheep" of the highway patrol administration at

this time. The administration had created the new Inspections and Standards Section to be commanded by Major Sturtz. His job was to travel throughout the state conducting inspections at the post level. This meant he was out of the office, out of headquarters much of the time. Many people who would have experienced the things Major Sturtz experienced during this low point in his career would have become bitter. They would have probably retired whether they were ready to or not. He was amazing and an inspiration. His personality and demeanor were always the same. He treated everyone with respect and kindness. The fact that he was a Major sharing an office space with a trooper had to be demeaning to him, but he never let it show.

Much later in my career, I was abruptly, without any warning, transferred from a position I very much enjoyed. Correspondence announcing my transfer was sent within minutes of me being notified. Memories of Major Sturtz and his demeanor at a low point in his career returned to me. I was determined that I would not become bitter and decided I would try to make the best of it and learn what I could in my new position. He had a very positive influence on how I reacted at this difficult time at the end of my career.

When Dave would share stories about this time in his life, he always began, "I sulked and pouted for about thirty seconds. I thought, 'The administration believes they are punishing me with this assignment, but I'm going to make it fun'."

Dave redefined the position, changed the name and did what he loved to do. He was out from behind a desk and in the field with the troopers. This story is not about all the details of the turbulent times in the Highway Patrol and the leadership. Dave could have given us all the details, the people involved, and what happened during these years. But Dave would not want the widows nor the families of those involved to be hurt by the stories or their view of their loved one to be tarnished from past events.

Dave found a way to handle his greatest career disappointment and become a positive influence on the Patrol. During this time Dave had the respect, but not the title. He became the person to whom troopers came to during these troubled times. He was the voice of reason and of hope.

> *"Consider it pure joy, my brothers,*
> *whenever you face trials of many kinds,*
> *because you know that the testing of your faith*
> *develops perseverance."*
> *(James 1:2, NIV)*

Through this great disappointment, Dave was able to persevere. He stayed true to who he was and on course. God blessed him later with a position he never dreamed of, becoming the first Inspector General for the State of Ohio. Because Dave had experienced disappointment, he was able to be of support to others who were hurt and whose careers were stalled during this administration.

Life Lesson

• Even when you do the right things, you will experience disappointment and trials. It is how you handle the struggles of life that shows your true character.

Death of Loved Ones

In the first chapter of this book, I shared Dave's testimony of faith. In that testimony, Dave talked about his experiences with death and the devastating loss of his grandson, J.C. In this chapter, I want to share about these deaths and how Dave experienced the loss of loved ones.

Dave was the son who lived in Ohio, and therefore, lived the closest in distance to his parents. He spent time driving back and forth between Pickerington and Coshocton caring for the needs of his parents. He loved being able to be there for his parents and give back to them.

As his dad declined, Dave remembered taking him to Spitler's Restaurant for lunch before taking his car to a car lot to be sold. His dad told him that it was time for him to stop driving. Now this was an emotional time for Dave and his dad. His dad loved cars and probably owned over 50 cars in his lifetime. Dave received his love for cars and driving from his dad, and now to see this chapter of his dad's life come to an end made Dave aware of the ending chapter of life.

Before Dave's dad died, he opened his eyes and told Dave, "Boy, I will be OK." He gave Dave a sense of peace about death. Dave always said that his mom died of a broken heart. She missed her Walter so much that she could not live without him. She died eleven months later.

Dave's love and respect for his parents did not end at their death. He continued to place flowers on their grave every year. But what gave his parents' lives purpose and meaning are the stories that Dave continued to tell about them and the difference they made in his life. They gave Dave and his brothers a firm foundation of values, morals, principles and faith upon which Dave built his life.

Dave's best friend, Chet Hayth, went through sixteen cancer surgeries and treatments. And as a friend, Dave was with Chet through each one of them. Dave spent countless hours sitting with Chet out back of Chet's house playing cribbage and listening to music. Some days they talked and some days they just sat together. Their friendship was so deep that words were not always needed. Dave walked with his friend through the dying and never wavered in his love and support.

Dave's first wife, Iris, was diagnosed with ovarian cancer. Together they walked the journey of treatments, surgeries, experimental studies, and the dying. Dave cared for Iris in their home the last months of her life. He took care of her through the night and worked during the day. In his 1989 calendar on June 10th, Dave wrote these words:

> Iris, my beloved wife passed away at 10:10 PM. This was after a gallant and courageous fight with ovarian cancer—7 operations, 4 chemos, 1 radiation treatment. A brave and wonderful Christian woman. —DDS

In a three-and-a-half-year period of time, all of these deaths occurred, including his mother-in-law. How did Dave make it through this time? Let me share his words:

> These deaths were staggering and overpowering, but with God's love, strength and compassion, I was able to support, to love and to care for all these people. God was truly a powerful force in my life who sustained me and continues to be a powerful force in my life.

Dave relied on the strength and power of God to walk with him through the dying and the death of the closest people in his life. He relied on the comfort and protection of God.

> *"Even though I walk*
> *through the valley of the shadow of death,*
> *I fear no evil, for thou art with me;*
> *thy rod and thy staff they comfort me."*
> *(Psalm 23:4, RSV)*

The one death that made Dave question God was the death of his eleven-month-old grandson, J.C. It didn't make sense then and still doesn't make sense. Dave recalls the event of that day that brought the depth of despair:

> Jim Sheridan (the funeral director) asked Sonny (Frank Block, the other grandfather) and me to carry the little white casket at the cemetery. Sonny and I picked up that casket. It wasn't heavy in weight, but it was the heaviest burden I have ever carried. Tears just streamed down my face. I was angry, hurt, crushed. It wasn't right. It wasn't fair. I felt the pain and burden of death.

It was through the faith of his grandson, Chris, who at age five had the childlike faith to believe and to know his brother was in heaven with Jesus that Dave came out of the darkness of death.

Dave walked with me through the death of my parents and many friends and family over the years of our marriage. When I became a hospice chaplain, Dave became a hospice volunteer. He had two very special people whom he visited as a volunteer, Curtis and Anne.

Dave spent time with Curtis and Anne for many months. He read Scripture with them and prayed with them. Anne would sing to him. It was her gift to him. They talked about their faith and heaven. Curtis couldn't talk but could communicate in gestures and grunts. Curtis was always excited to see Dave, and they spent time just being together. In these visits, Dave connected heart to heart and walked the journey with two people from different backgrounds and walks of life.

Dave had witnessed deaths throughout his Highway Patrol career. He was the last person to see some people alive after an accident. Dave witnessed mangled bodies with detached parts, and he saw the blood of tragedies. He held the hand of a person and heard their last words.

Dave taught a Sunday School class at Reynoldsburg United Methodist Church years ago entitled, "Death, Where is Your Sting?" based on the scripture from 1 Corinthians 15:

> Death is swallowed up in victory. O death, where is thy victory? O death, where is thy sting? The sting of death is sin, and the power of sin is the

law. But thanks be to God, who gives us victory through our Lord Jesus Christ. (1 Corinthians 15:55-57, RSV)

In this class, Dave organized speakers to share about death from their professional perspective. He invited a doctor, nurse, funeral home director, minister and even Dave himself came one Sunday in uniform to share from the law enforcement perspective. Dave wanted the class to recognize that death is a part of life. It depends upon your frame of reference how you view death and your understanding of faith.

Dave had witnessed death through those he loved, through his career, through being married to a minister, and through volunteering with hospice. Life was different after each death. Dave learned to live in the different and learn from each experience. Death made an impact in his life and through his stories, he kept the memories of those who came before him.

All of these deaths prepared Dave for the journey of his own death.

Life Lesson

- Death is a part of life. It is finding meaning and purpose in the lives of those we love and telling the stories of their lives. Recognize that within us is a memory of those with whom we have journeyed through life.

The Accidents

Dave was in a severe car accident the first year of his Highway Patrol career in 1959.

> I had graduated on June 26, 1959 from the Academy and was stationed at Lisbon. I was working Thanksgiving, November 26, 1959. I slowed down for the traffic signal on Route 14, and I was struck from behind by a vehicle. My trunk was in the back seat of the car. The driver and passenger in the vehicle that hit me were injured and taken to the hospital. I got out of my car to put fuzees out and wait for the tow truck. I leaned down to strike them against the pavement. I must have passed out because when I woke up I was flat on the pavement. I had two fuzees in my hands. I couldn't stand up. My back went out on me. So, I crawled using the fuzees to pull me forward. They were sharp on one end, and I dug into the pavement and pulled my body. I tore my pants and shirt but made it to my patrol car. I tried to pull myself up to open the door and finally did. I radioed for help. The Pennsylvania Trooper got to me first because I was only three miles from the PA border. I was in the Salem City Hospital in traction for three weeks. I had dislocated and crushed discs in my back.

> When they released me, the doctors wanted me to just begin walking and take it slow and easy. Iris left for work, and I slowly began. I would get out of bed and slowly walk around the apartment. Then I would walk the steps. The next day I would walk more. Then I tried one push up, then the next day another. But I kept pushing myself. I

did my own therapy, built myself back into shape and in six months I was back at the Academy as PT instructor.

Dave did not allow an accident to slow him down. He worked, trained and struggled through the pain. He persevered until he was back doing what he loved. Dave had back issues all his life as a result of this accident, but he persevered through it.

While Dave was District 1 Commander in the State Highway Patrol, three State Troopers from the Findlay District were killed.

I was Commander for three days and Lieutenant Jim Kirkendall was coming back from a physical in Columbus. He was involved in a traffic crash with a truck and was killed. *(October 28, 1970)*

Joel Miller, a sub-post guy in Hardin County, went home to eat lunch with his pregnant wife and two little boys. He left there and fifteen minutes later a train ran over him and killed him. *(December 6, 1971)*

In 1973, I had a brand-new trooper, David Sterner. His mom and dad came from Massillon to eat breakfast with him on a Sunday morning. They left to go back. He waved to his mom and dad. He was working Highway 15 and was going north. He saw a speeder and turned around. He was going about 90 mph. A retired school teacher pulled out at Route 37 and he sheared off the front of her car. She wasn't hurt but his car flipped. He hit a culvert and his car caught fire. I was called and was there within seven minutes. When I got there his ammunition was going off. I couldn't do anything. That's what got me. I couldn't help. The first person who came was Colonel Chiaramonte asking, "What do you need?" When he came, I was okay. *(February 25, 1973)*

These trooper deaths made a profound impact on Dave's life and family. His daughter, Gretchen, recalls the deaths of the Troopers:

I was in fourth and fifth grades. What I remember was it shook Dad to the core. I remember him being so sad and I knew part of his heart broke. I think he felt helpless, but there was nothing he could have done. It was quiet in our house for weeks. After the death of Trooper Sterner, dad started telling us that we would be okay if anything happened to him.

Life Lesson

• Accidents happen. People die doing their jobs. It's not fair. It is learning from it that matters.

CHAPTER 11

JUST BEING ME

Sense of Humor

"A cheerful heart is a good medicine,
but a downcast spirit dries up the bones."
(Proverbs 17:22, RSV)

Dave was known for his sense of humor, his stories and his laughter. In a gathering of friends, Sunday School class or family at our home, it didn't take long to hear laughter from Dave and the beginning of a story. He loved to joke with people, but he never made fun of anyone. Most of his stories were about his own adventures. He was willing to share his misadventures if they would teach another person what not to do. He loved to joke around with people. His son, Craig and Dave used to pull some amazing April Fool's Day jokes on one another. They finally had to call a truce in the last year of Dave's life.

Dave pulled this prank on his mom. Here is the story in Dave's words:

> My mom entered every contest you can imagine, always hoping to win the grand prize. While on the Highway Patrol and stationed in Lisbon, Ohio, I called my Mom and disguised my voice. In a very excited voice and talking very fast, I asked my Mom if her name was Helene Sturtz. Did she live at 1602 Beach Avenue, Coshocton, Ohio? She of course, responded, "Yes." I told her she had won the grand prize. I heard her yell at my dad, "Walter, I've won the grand prize." Then she very quickly asked, "What is the grand prize?" Still in my fake voice, I told her it was a car. I heard her

171

loudly explain to my dad, "My God, Walter, I've won a car." She was yelling and screaming with excitement. I then tried to tell her it was me, her son, David. In her excitement she didn't hear me the first five or six times. Finally, she realized it was me and she was so disappointed that she hung up on me. When I tried to call back, they wouldn't answer the phone. It took my mom years before she laughed about it, but it wasn't really funny to her. I was just trying to be funny and it backfired.

Little things made Dave laugh. The funniest times were when he would get tickled at himself and laugh. That was the best laughter of all. Little boys and big boys all seem to think bodily functions and body noises are the funniest. They don't seem to outgrow it. One day I commented to Dave that he seemed to say "poop" every day. So, from then on, every day he would ask me, "Did I say poop today?" and I would reply, "You just did." Every night when we went to bed, I would turn out the light and Dave would say, "It's poop dark." I still say it every night!

"Then we were filled with laughter,
and we sang happy songs."
(Psalm 126:2, NCV)

To be present when Dave laughed, you had to laugh with him. His whole body laughed. He could laugh until he cried or made you cry from laughing so hard. His arms and legs would move as he laughed and shared a story. Laughter is truly good medicine for the soul.

Life Lesson

- Laugh! Laugh every day! Don't take yourself so seriously!

Nicknames

"Then Andrew took Simon to Jesus.
Jesus looked at him and said,
'You are Simon son of John. You shall be called Cephas.'
('Cephas' means Peter.)"
(John 1:42, RSV)

My name was given to me by my mother. She chose David because the definition is "beloved." My middle name is Dale, and my mom always joked it was for Dale Evans, Roy Roger's sidekick.

In high school, my nickname was "Sturtzee." The athletes in high school called me "The Hawk" because wherever the ball was, I was there. At the University of Cincinnati, my nickname was "The Preacher" because I didn't smoke, drink or run with the wild college girls. My Grandma Kubic called me "Davey Dale."

In the State Highway Patrol, Dave was known as *"The Major"* because he was a major for thirteen years and out of respect for his contribution to the Patrol. He was also called "DD" and "733" for his unit number. After being the first Inspector General, Dave was also called *"The General"* by those in State Government.

Dave was also known as *"The Legend"* of the State Highway Patrol. He had a unique career. He was the person who connected the old guard with the new. He knew the old timers and trained the new ones. His time of riot training added to this nickname.

Dave received one nickname from former Governor James Rhodes.

> I was on detail at the Governor's residence for the wedding of his daughter. The Governor wanted troopers that were tall and looked the part. It was a hot summer day and we were all sweating in our wool shirts. The Governor walked by and asked my name. I told him and he asked where I was from. I said, "Coshocton."
>
> He came back later with lemonade and said, "Here have something to drink."
>
> I said, "I'm on duty, sir."
>
> "I know that, and I am ordering you to have a drink, Coshocton kid." And when I would encounter the Governor from then on, he called me "The Coshocton Kid."

The nickname that made Dave smile and feel blessed was that of *"Grandpa"* and *"Pop."* He loved being a Grandfather and Great-Grandfather. His oldest great-granddaughter, Brooklyn, gave him the name *"Pop."* She just looked at him one day before she was two and said, *"Pop."*

Not only did Dave have nicknames, he nicknamed almost everyone in his family. His daughter, Gretchen was named *"Dretchen."* His son, Craig was *"Craigo."* His grandson Chris was *"Chris Dave"* and when he was younger was called *"Skeezik."* His other grandson, O'Shay, was nicknamed *"The Bird."* Our first dog, Specs, whose official name was *"Inspector General II"* was also nicknamed *"Pudboy"* or *"Puddy."* Our most recent dog, Annie, received her name because we got her on our Anniversary. She is also called *"Annie Girl."*

All of these names given by Dave to those he loved were terms of endearment. He nicknamed those he loved out of his affection for them. It was Dave's way of expressing the special bond. All the names given to Dave by others expressed their respect and relationship with him. They were given to express the qualities others saw in him, and also to have a special connection to him. God calls us by name too. We are his children. Dave loved being called a child of God.

Life Lesson

- Your name connects you to others. Your nickname is their perception of you.

Hugs

"You protect people in the shadow of your wings."
(Psalm 36:7, NCV)

Dave was known for his hugs. They were big bear hugs that took you in and you felt safe and protected and loved. You knew you were hugged when you received a hug from Dave and then a kiss on the cheek. My first encounter with Dave was his hug. I did not grow up in a family that hugged, but I became a hugger in my ministry and even more so through my marriage to Dave. He expressed his love outwardly, and it was received with the same grace it was given.

"My favorite thing about Dave was his hugs."

—Mary Kay Laner

"In a meeting with Dave, along with brothers Don and Jim at Dave and Elaine's home, we gathered for one last time to say 'goodbye' as Dave's condition became graver. When it came time to leave, Dave struggled to stand from his chair, I told him to stay seated, but he said, 'No, I'll stand to give you a hug'."

—Ken Sturtz

Dave always greeted his brothers with a hug and a kiss on the cheek, and he did the same before they left. This last hug and kiss on the cheek was a very emotional time for all the brothers. Dave stood out of love like he always did. Nothing was going to change that for him.

Dave's hug and a kiss on the cheek were worth waiting for, and widows at church would form a line to receive a hug. Dave spent much of his time before and after worship services hugging people. It didn't matter their age, gender or station in life, Dave would hug. It was always interesting to watch Dave hug people who were not huggers. After a while, Dave made them huggers. Sometimes he would say to a person, "Let me teach you how to hug."

Dave had the gift of touch. It was always appropriate and given with compassion, respect and the love of God. That was Dave. So many people tell me they miss his hugs. Me too!

Life Lesson

- Hug! Show that you love someone today. Hug them!

Dave-isms

Dave had a way with words, not just in writing letters and telling stories, but in how he phrased sentences and put words together. He had a unique way of saying things to get your attention and so you would remember what he said. He also had some sayings that he spoke on a regular basis. For example:

"You irritate the snot out of me." Spoken when he was upset and angry.

"I'll eat the dregs." The dregs was what he called what is at the bottom of the cereal box, what is left. He would always eat all of the crumbs.

"We made a 'plete circle." Dave would say this after the end of a trip and we arrived home. He said he got this from his dad.

"I feel punko." This is what Dave would say when he felt sick.

"Where you be?" When I would come home, he would ask this question.

"Aim low boys, they're riding short-legged ponies." Be aware of the unexpected. This was engraved on his plaque from Homeland Security when he retired.

"If you are wearing spurs, don't squat." Be aware of yourself and your surroundings.

"Do you hear me?" Making sure you are paying attention.

"It's whipper-jawed." It was messed up or crooked.

"I'll beat the drum and you will row." Spoken at the Academy when cadets were not doing what they

should be doing. Dave was the leader and they were to follow what was expected.

"It is what it is." An acceptance when you can't change it.

"A bird must have pooped on the line." Spoken whenever the electricity went out.

"That's minutiae." One of Dave's favorite words he used to describe when people would get caught up in trivial details of something and not see what was important.

Oh, there are so many more. I hope that those who knew Dave and are reading this will remember more from your encounters with Dave. The little things that make a person unique are what we remember, and what lives on after they are gone. When you remember something they said, it should bring a smile to your face and a thanksgiving in your heart that they lived.

Dave also would change lyrics in songs when he sang them. He would make up something that was totally not in the song. He used to ruin so many songs for me because I would remember his lyrics, not the original ones.

Dave's favorite song was *The Third Man Theme* from the movie *The Third Man*. He loved the zither from the original score. He would always say, *"I'm the third man."* It was a 1949 British film of intrigue, mystery and investigation. "The Third Man Theme" was played on the organ by Chuck Yannerella at Dave's funeral as the casket was wheeled into the worship center. This was at Dave's request. He felt the song described a part of him.

Dave's favorite movies were *The Last of the Mohicans* and *Red River*. He loved the cowboy movies and had a heart for the Native American Indians. He read all the western novels and collected Indian artifacts. He could name Native American chiefs and tell their stories.

Dave's favorite food was eggs. I think one reason was because he knew how to make eggs. He made them every way possible. His favorite way was over easy with toast. Toast was his "go to" snack when he was hungry and didn't know what to eat. It was easy and fast to make. Anyone who had ever been around Dave when he was hungry knew the importance of quick. Dave turned "mean" when he was hungry, or at least that is how I would describe it.

He had "the look." Every mom has "the look" according to their children and you know you are in trouble. Dave had "the look" that said, *"I know"* or *"I am on to you."* He always said he had no idea that he had a certain look. One day I captured it in a picture, and we determined it was his Inspector General look. When Dave gave the look, you did not want it to be directed toward you.

Dave had no ability to build or repair anything. His idea of repair was to use a hammer and pound it into submission. He loved to buy tools, but not use them. Dave had an agreement with our friend and handyman, Ron. Ron did the remodeling and repairs, and Dave did the investigations. This was an excellent agreement between them!

Dave had some OCD in him. He had to put the sock and shoe on his left foot first and then the sock and shoe on his right foot. He could not put both socks on and then his shoes. The socks also had a left and right foot. If you unfolded the socks, the top sock went on the left foot. He always said if he had to run in an emergency, at least he had one shoe on. He always straightened pairs of shoes. They had to be together. When he lifted hand weights and set them down, they had to be straight together. He always had to go out the same door he came in when going to any event, home or function.

These are just some of the quirks that made Dave unique. We all have habits, favorite things, and terminology we use. When we remember people, we recall these special quirks, and we smile as we describe the things that stand out about them. Sometimes we even recognize that we have picked up the trait. I notice I straighten shoes and hand weights just like Dave. These little quirks or OCD traits that bothered me during our marriage are what I remember now and they bring a smile. These are the daily living reminders of Dave's life.

Life Lesson

- Don't be like everybody else. Have your own style and way of expressing yourself.

Collector of Things

Dave inherited from his mom the love of collecting things and knickknacks. Dave had many collections during our married life. He discovered the Red Barn Flea Market and began collecting brass. Anything brass. We had all types of brass animals, keys, containers, and knobs. He collected American Indian artifacts, pictures and books. Books were his biggest collection, because Dave loved to read. He read daily, and in his retirement, he read hundreds of books. I have index cards of several hundred books that he read. He would write out a card for each book.

Dave loved a good pen. Whenever he went to the bank or a funeral home and he liked the pen, he would take it. He always said they have lots of pens. He had dozens of pens because he was always writing letters, notes, or reports. He wrote out everything before it was typed. He used two fingers to type, so after we were married I became his typist. He wrote everything on legal pads. The rough draft of this book was written on legal pads I still had from Dave. He also used page protectors for every speech, every article he saved and every picture. He would make notebooks for articles he saved. I have hundreds of page protectors in my office closet.

Dave always had about six pairs of athletic shoes. He used one to walk in, one pair were his *"kick abouts"* as he called them. He would wear another pair to go places, and one pair for the yard. He always kept a pair or two in shoe boxes on the shelf of his closet just in case he needed them. He always said, "You can't have too many running shoes."

The one collection that began in our marriage was the collection of rocks. When we purchased a property for his son, it was surrounded by farm fields. We began walking the fields and bringing back rocks. I'm not talking small rocks. I'm talking rocks that weighed more than thirty-five pounds, and many rocks that took two people to carry or a John Deere gator to haul. We would bring them back to our yard and decorate with rocks. In each of our moves, we moved the rocks first.

I have shared many of Dave's collections with his friends and family. I wanted them to have a physical reminder of Dave. At the Sunday School class Christmas Party after Dave's death, I gave each person a brass key from Dave's collection. It was to remind them that the key to Dave's life was his faith in Jesus.

I am not a collector of knickknacks. I continue to give away and share what I have with those around me. I enjoy pictures and have many scrapbooks filled with memories. I take out the picture books and remember. I have Dave's letters that I can re-read and remember the love we shared.

This book is written from the memories collected over the years. The stories, the speeches, the articles, the pictures and most importantly the difference Dave's life made in my life and the lives around him. The material possessions we own from loved ones trigger memories.

Life Lesson

- The memories that come from possessions are a treasure.

Documentation

*"And he said, 'Write this,
for these words are trustworthy and true.'"
(Revelation 21:5, RSV)*

Dave documented everything. He time stamped and dated every letter, communication and piece of paper he received in the mail. I still have his stamps that say, "Completed," "Priority," "Draft" and "Copy" which he used daily in his investigative work.

His calendars were filled with appointments for his work, but also reminders to pick up dry cleaning, doctors and dentist appointments and oil changes. But when you begin to read through his calendars, they were more a daily diary of his life. He listed when babies were born, weddings, funerals and vacations. The calendars are about relationships more than days of the year listing major life events. I have shared his calendar entries from the death of his wife, Iris, and from the beginning of our relationship. His calendars were the joys and sorrows of life in the midst of work and daily errands.

My calendars have always had my schedule listed, but because of how much information I have found on Dave's calendars, I have begun to write more about the events and people in each day. It has become more of a journal of my life than just dates.

Dave also documented phone calls. He kept records in his work of all phone calls. Even at home, he would write on a piece of paper the date, time and person calling and notes of the conversation. I never kept these notes, but if I had they would have documented his relationship and connection with people.

The days of the year are more than dates on a calendar you cross off. The days are landmarks of our relationships. The dates represent the lives of people we encountered that day and the difference they made in our life. Dates are significant.

Dave could remember dates and times. He also had great recall in the stories he told. He remembered people's names and something significant about them. When he saw the person again, he would remember previous conversations and inquire about a concern they had shared previously or about someone in their family. Dave paid attention to the details in other people's lives. This is a gift. It is about listening with the intent to learn about the person. People who have confidence in who they are and do not need others to build them up tend to have this quality. It is being humble and not needing others to know all about you.

Dave would say about conversations he had, "I learned all kinds of details about the person, but all they know about me is my name."

This gift was part investigative skill and part his love and compassion for people. He didn't focus on himself but on others.

Life Lesson

- Write down the events of daily life. Make your calendar about relationships, not just dates and appointments.

Lawn Mowing

No story about David Sturtz is complete without sharing about mowing the lawn. Dave used to tell about how he mowed the lawn when he lived in Chevington Woods:

> My neighbor had a riding lawn mower, but I had a push mower. I would put weights around my ankles and a waist weight belt and some days a weighted vest and make mowing the lawn a workout. I would start about the same time as my neighbor and finish before him. I worked up a sweat while he was just riding.

Dave did buy a riding lawn mower while living there and would always see how fast he could mow. He always had to make a pattern in the lawn. He had a method to how he mowed. He never liked clumps of grass in the lawn. He would mow high and then lower the blade and mow the lawn again. When we moved to Saylor Road with two and a half acres to mow, mowing took on a whole other purpose. For Dave, lawn mowing became his alone time and prayer time. He would mow two to three times a week whether the grass needed it or not. It was not about the grass anymore, it was about his alone time and quiet time to think and talk to God.

Life Lesson

- Find your alone time with God in whatever form that works for you.

CHAPTER 12

THE COMPLETION OF EARTHLY LIFE

The Beginning of the Journey Home

D ave began having vision issues in the late fall of 2014. He had an appointment with our family optometrist who scheduled him to see a specialist. We made an appointment and the earliest available was February 11, 2015. One evening on the drive home, Dave almost ran into the ditch on the road where we lived. He became angry that I yelled for him to turn the wheel or we would be in the ditch. To him, we were fine. I began seeing other issues, and we determined it would be best for him not to drive until after his specialist appointment. This was very difficult for Dave at first. He had spent his career driving, and now he had to have someone drive him. He felt this was only temporary. He would have some type of eye surgery and then he would be fine.

We took a short vacation at the end of January, 2015, to visit friends in Florida. Dave's vision became worse. He could not walk a straight line crossing the street or down the sidewalk. He had to hold onto my arm as he walked. He had his appointment with the ophthalmologist on February 11, 2015. He was sent to the Emergency Room for an MRI where the brain tumors were discovered.

Dave was first told by an ER doctor while he was alone that he had brain cancer. It took his breath away. It was like a gut punch to the stomach. Then we were told the tumors were benign and slow growing. Yes, slow growing but they had been growing for years and no longer had room to grow in the brain. His head was full of tumors. The shock of this news left Dave and me and the family numb for a time. We had lots of questions and what the next steps of action needed to be.

> When I first found out about the tumors, I was thinking how come they can't take them out or give me medicine. The surgeon said there was nothing he could do. The tumors were throughout my entire brain. I said in this day and age you mean there is nothing. He said, 'I'm a surgeon and if I could do something, I would have cut on you yesterday.' He told me that how my tumors were that he couldn't take them out because I wouldn't survive surgery. For a while it stunned me. Each time I'd see him, I'd ask, 'Are you sure?' He would say, 'Yes.' I'm just fortunate that the tumors grew in the back of my head, and I can't see them.

The surgeon told us the tumors were slow-growing and could not be taken out without affecting all parts of the body. He told Dave to live his life to the fullest. The tumors probably had been growing for years. In the last month of Dave's life, he was on hospice care. He was able to travel in July to visit his oldest brother, Don, his wife, Alice, and their family. He had a great visit and did very well on the trip. We had planned to visit his other two brothers, but Dave was unable to make the trips. So, the three brothers came to Dave on the weekend of August 14th and 15th. They had a wonderful visit together. Dave shared with them very honestly:

> I don't know how long. I don't know what time I have. I'm thankful I have time to say good bye. The hospice people assured me they would do

everything to help me with pain. I don't want to leave this house. I want it to end here.

Dave's determination and strength was evident to the end:

I made up my mind that every day, I'm going to get up no matter what. I'm going to stand. I don't want to cry. It's hard not to cry. I've made up my mind that if there is any strength in me, I'm going to get up.

And Dave got up every day but his last day on earth. Dave had walked the journey of dying with his first wife, Iris, and was her caregiver. Now he was the one being cared for. He had witnessed the grace and faith of Iris as she traveled this journey. He had held the hand of parents and friends on the journey. He accepted that it was his time to take the journey. Oh, there were struggles and tears because of the deep love and not wanting to leave those he loved.

Life Lesson

- How do you deal with devastating news when you are face to face with your own mortality? Dave faced the end with the same foundation of faith, love and integrity that he lived life. Great example. Great life lesson.

Glimpses of Heaven

Dave had a biopsy performed of his tumors and skull to determine the type of tumors. He was diagnosed with meningioma. He had a long incision in the back of his head that became infected in March which led to another hospitalization. It was during this hospital stay that Dave had a dream of heaven.

> I looked at the clock and it was 2 a.m., and I fell asleep. I think I dreamed, but it seemed so real. I was walking down this beautiful path. Everything was brilliant in color. There were flowers and trees. I was walking and felt such warmth and peace. I felt someone with me, but I just saw all this beauty around me. Then I was stopped by what felt like a Plexiglas wall. I could see through it, but I couldn't go forward. I heard or maybe felt a voice saying, "You can't go any further. You need to go back. It's not your time yet." Then I awoke in my hospital bed. I looked at the clock and it was 4 am. I had been in heaven for two hours.

I remember walking into Dave's hospital room that morning and seeing his excitement and eagerness to tell me what had just happened to him. He was more alert and accepting after this encounter.

God continued to give him glimpses of the future. He was visited by angels. Several months before Dave died, he asked me if I saw her. I asked, "Who?"

He said, "The girl sitting on the sofa."

"No, I don't see anyone." I replied. This happened later in the week, and several more times the next week.

Roger Solt was with Dave in one of these encounters:

> We were sitting in his great room, and he suddenly said, "Do you see her? She is right here beside me." I replied that I could not see her. Dave got a real serious look on his face and said, "Elaine can't see her either."

After a few of these encounters, I realized that God was sending an angel to be with Dave to prepare him for the journey. Dave was able to describe her:

> She is about thirteen or fourteen years old. She is
> blonde with a gap between her two front teeth.
> She is wearing a blue blouse and dark blue
> pantaloons. She doesn't say anything, but just sits
> there and looks at me. She doesn't scare me. She is
> peaceful.

Dave and I talked about these encounters. I believe
God was sending the angel who would eventually take
him to heaven. God was allowing Dave to feel
comfortable with her and not be afraid when it was time
to go to heaven.

Because Dave was an investigator and always
seeking truth and the facts, I believe God gave him a
vision of heaven because Dave needed the facts to be
assured. I believe Dave also received the vision of his
angel for the same reason. In Hebrews 1:14 (RSV), we
read, "Are not all angels ministering spirits sent to serve
those who will inherit salvation?"

Dave always was looking for the facts and the proof,
and the angel was sent for that reason. God blessed Dave
with the proof he needed so that he was not afraid. The
angel went away for several months. I believe that God
sent the angel to prepare Dave and to be comfortable
with her, and when it was time to go to heaven she
would return. She returned a little over a week before
Dave died. She would sit on his bed and just be present.
One day, she brought with her an older woman. Dave
described her as wearing a "babushka" on her head, and
she was very quiet.

Dave had a second experience with heaven. Tom
Rice and Rob Hartsell were with Dave the Wednesday

before he died. Dave went into a coma-like state with shallow breathing. Tom and Rob thought Dave was dying, and I received a call to come quickly. In the few minutes it took for me to drive home, Dave started to come out of the coma-like state and began to talk a little. He was a little agitated that he was back in his bed and not in heaven.

After Tom and Rob left and Dave settled down, he told me that he had gone to heaven again. "It was beautiful. It was filled with brilliant and bright colors. It was so peaceful and I felt so good. When can I go back?"

In my book, *Living in the Different*, I share about Dave's visions of heaven and angels. God blessed Dave with the reassurance he needed so that he could die in peace. Dave had no doubt about heaven, but now he had the assurance that he was going to a wonderful place. It gave me and all of those who knew the story of his experiences, the hope and peace of heaven.

This whole experience was a life lesson and an affirmation that there is a Heaven and Dave is there.

The Last Chapter of Life

Dave was a people person. He had friends from all chapters of his life who remained important to him. He loved telling stories and sharing life lessons with people. He lived life always interacting with people and knowing what was going on in the lives of people around him. Therefore, why would his dying be any different than his living? It may have been easier for me to care for Dave by myself and just have the family around him instead of coordinating a schedule of people to be with him. But that would not have been right nor would that have been Dave. Dave was able to teach life lessons and share stories in his dying.

I organized our Sunday School class to be with Dave while I was at work, prepare meals as needed and even had several who came to sing to Dave. Dave had visits from friends on the Highway Patrol and from other chapters of his life. Here are a few stories:

> "Dave and I continued to meet weekly as share partners even when he was not feeling great. He shared his thoughts about his life on earth coming to a close and how he felt about that. He looked forward to seeing Jesus. It occurred to me that Dave was showing many people who visited him in his final days how to die gracefully."
>
> —Roger Solt

> "I am so glad you and Dave allowed us in your home to help. Guy and Dave had a wonderful conversation that allowed Guy to realize how God was always working in Dave's life. I had time to tell Dave 'Love you, Dave.' 'You too, Deb' just like a brother. What a wonderful gift for an only child."
>
> —Guy and Debbie Harmon

> "In Dave's final days, I was able to meet with him twice. He said, 'I am ok with all of this.' I knew that his faith was a comfort to him. Dave set an example for me to follow. He was strong, forgiving and a servant to others."
>
> —Tom Eich

"The last time I had the privilege of connecting with Dave and the last time I had a chance to give that amazing man a hug was at my grandfather's wake. Dave was battling tumors and while he walked with a cane this time, he still had that sweet smile and undoubted kindness in his eyes. It was that kindness and love that he shared with me throughout my life that gave me the strength to make it through that day. My final memory of Dave is etched in my mind. There was a moment during the wake when Dave saluted the man who had raised me, one last time. It was one of the most humbling and sincere moments in my life."

—Scott Walsh

Dave had the opportunity to say good bye and to hear words from those whom he loved. He heard *"I love you"* and *"Thank you"* and *"You made a difference in my life."* He heard that his life had purpose and meaning. He heard that others saw his faith in God by the way he lived. He heard that people learned from his stories and life lessons. Dave's life was focused on relationships and his dying was focused on relationships.

In the last weekend he spent with his brothers, Dave said, *"I am blessed."* Dave recognized the blessings of his life. Life was not perfect, but it was blessed by God. He was grateful for all the experiences of his life. It was difficult to hug his brothers, say *"I love you"* and give them a kiss on the cheek knowing it would be the last time here on earth. The bond of love remains always for the Sturtz brothers.

Dave had the opportunity to say good bye to his children, grandchildren, great-granddaughters, his dear friends and many people from church. The one very emotional good bye was with the Ricket family. The Sturtz Family and the Ricket Family were a combined family. We shared holidays together, and Dave felt a responsibility to the three daughters, Allison, Ashley and Abby. In the final good bye, Dave was not speaking but had tears in his eyes as he looked at them and loved them.

Dave taught in his dying. He shared not so much in words but in receiving the love in the last days that he had shared. It came full circle.

Legacy

"Keep your roots deep in him and have your lives built on him.
Be strong in the faith, just as you were taught,
and always be thankful."
(Colossians 2:7, NCV)

Dave recognized that God had a special calling for his life:

> I believe God allowed me to serve and protect through my career on the Highway Patrol and my years as Ohio Inspector General. God gave me special gifts of communication, writing skills, and being able to solve complex problems and to do all these with ethics, morals and principles.

Dave's legacy was not just in the work accomplished but in how he did his work and how he treated others. Dave lived by an ethical standard that was rooted in his faith. He was a man of integrity.

His brother, Don, shared with Dave about his legacy in their last visit together: "Your life has been worthwhile. Your life mattered. People have changed because of your influence."

I received a letter from Abby Ricket shortly after Dave's funeral. Abby was influenced by Dave and recognized his legacy:

> You and Dave are like a second set of parents to me. I have always looked up to both of you so much. I remember in school being asked who my role models were and I always thought of you and Dave. I am so grateful you have been a part of my life. When I left Dave's funeral, I felt inspired. The stories about Dave and the message that was conveyed multiple times about him being a strong Christian and always doing what was ethical really stuck with me. I've always known this about Dave, but seeing how many people he left an impact on made me realize how great his legacy is. I hope to leave a legacy like Dave and you.

Abby grew up around Dave and was part of the youth ministry where I served. Dave's life made a difference in her. She represents many youths who were influenced by Dave and are now strong Christian adults making a difference. Dave's legacy is in how these young people are living their lives for Jesus and doing what is ethical and having a foundation.

Dave lived in the world of law enforcement fighting evil and corruption. He could have become cynical, but he stayed positive and strong in his faith. He said going to church and being in Sunday School balanced him in his life. He saw the dark side in his work but saw the hope and good especially when teaching the youth Sunday School class. He had hope in the future.

Dave completed his earthly journey. He completed the number of days laid out for him as Scripture tells us in Psalm 139:16 (NIV), "All the days ordained for me were written in your book before one of them came to be." Dave's influence, though, continues to live on through his words, his actions and how he lived his life. His life continues to bear fruit in the people he influenced whether known by him personally or reading these words.

There is a lot of David D. Sturtz in me. I acquired some of his quirks by living with him. The little things Dave did still linger within me. He enhanced my life and helped strengthen my confidence and smooth out some rough edges of my life. The legacy is the love that will never die. Dave's love lives on within my heart forever.

Life Lesson

- We learn from those we follow. Choose wisely whom you follow. Find the good qualities in others and develop them within you. A piece of each person who has touched our lives is within us. That is their legacy.

Heaven

God blessed Dave with a glimpse of heaven through his dreams, visions and angel visits. Dave had faith and believed in heaven all his life. Dave knew heaven was real even though he never saw it. That is what faith is.

"Faith means being sure of the things we hope for
and knowing that something is real even if we do not see it."
(Hebrews 11:1, NCV)

Dave's faith matured in the last months of his life. He looked forward with hope, leaving this world of pain and going to heaven. He was sad and very emotional about leaving all of us whom he loved. But he had hope of being reunited with those he loved in heaven and seeing Jesus face to face.

"But we are hoping for something we do not have yet,
and we are waiting for it patiently."
(Romans 8:25, NCV)

God gave Dave this assurance that the end of this earthly life was just the beginning of life eternal. This assurance was for all of us who knew Dave and are reading these words. This world is not all there is. God has prepared a place for all of us who believe. Jesus gives us this promise:

> "In my Father's house are many rooms; if it were not so, would I have told you that I go to prepare a place for you? And when I go and prepare a place for you, I will come again and will take you to myself, that where I am you may be also." (John 14:2-3, RSV)

Dave was certain of heaven. He had been given personal assurances throughout his life. One day after his dad had died, Dave was in the basement of his own home and heard his dad's voice say, *"Boy, I'm okay. It's beautiful here."* His wife, Iris, believed she was going to have some type of job in heaven, and they talked together about it. Dave heard all my stories from hospice patients and in ministry, people who experienced a moment of heaven on earth.

The joy for Dave is that he was welcomed into heaven with the words, "Well done good and faithful servant, enter into the joy of your Master." (Matthew 25:21, RSV) The sadness is for us that he is no longer physically with us. The hope is that someday we will be reunited in heaven, and that sustains me. The belief that he has an eternal body free from pain brings me peace.

"Blessed are the dead who die in the Lord....
they will rest from their labor, for their deeds will follow them."
(Revelation 14:13, NIV)

THE NEXT CHAPTER

This is not the conclusion, but the beginning of the next chapter of influence in the life of David D. Sturtz. This book has been filled with life lessons and real-life stories. Oh, so many stories were left untold, but a flavor of his life and stories were shared. Dave found purpose and meaning in the stories of his life. My hope is that the stories of David D. Sturtz have influenced you and challenged you in leaving a legacy of your own for future generations.

Each person we encounter in life has a perspective in how they view other people's lives. They look through the lenses of their own worldview. Some saw Dave as intimidating while others saw his compassion and being approachable. Some saw Dave as bigger than life and could accomplish anything in his *"push, pull or get the hell out of the way"* attitude. Others saw his servant heart that hugged the widows and played with the two-year-old. Some saw Dave as hard, unbending and always right, while others saw his vulnerability and grace.

Dave was all of these perspectives and more. The perceptions and interpretations of his life are different for each person he influenced and in whose lives he made a difference. Dave shared life, lived life and experienced life. He never sat on the sidelines in sports nor in life. Dave was willing to open himself up to others. He loved, he challenged, he failed, he persevered and most of all he gave all he had and left it on the field of life.

One of Dave's leadership statements was *"Listen to me, trust me, follow me, and I will get you there and I will get you back."* In following, we recognize that Dave had a strong foundation of values, morals, ethics, and right and wrong. He was grounded in his faith in Jesus Christ.

"The secret is Christ himself, who is in you.
He is our only hope for glory."
(Colossians 1:27, NCV)

Jesus lived in the heart of Dave. He built upon this foundation of faith by adding his personality, his character, his determination and his confidence in who he was. All of this allowed Dave to stand strong and never compromise his integrity. But most of all, Dave followed Jesus to the cross. Jesus is our greatest Leader who sacrificed his life for our sins. Jesus said, "Follow me." Dave followed Jesus, and now he is in heaven with Jesus.

Dave's earthly life is complete, but the fruit of his labor continues. How David D. Sturtz lives on in our lives will give purpose and meaning to his life. Even if you did not know Dave personally and have only read about him, his life has made an impact through his words and stories. We are better people because he lived and loved. He continues to inspire us with his stories and his words.

This book has described a life well lived. Dave was not perfect. He had his faults and failures, but those died with him. What lives on is his love, his character and the fruit of his labor. It is now time for you to inspect the fruit and see how it has made a difference in your life and enhanced your life.

It is also a challenge to begin to bear fruit of your own to enhance the lives of those who come after you. It is time to recognize the fruit of the labor of those who have come before you and to name their influence so as to give meaning and purpose to those lives.

The question for you today is—For what would you like to be remembered? It is the quiet work we do in the lives of people that will live on after we are gone. What are you pouring into the lives of people around you? Hopefully, it is love that lives on, because love never dies.

> *"But tell the coming generation*
> *the glorious deeds of the Lord."*
> *(Psalm 78:4, RSV)*

It is fitting to conclude this book with the words of Dave's oldest brother, Don. It was Don who influenced Dave to accept Christ into his heart and life and was Dave's example for his own life.

> "No amount of writing could summarize the impact of Dave's life on those with whom he came in contact. Countless Ohioans benefitted from the contributions he made to the Ohio State Highway Patrol and to the Office of The Inspector General of Ohio and through his involvement in churches. Jim, Ken, and I miss his sense of humor and hearty laughter. While we no longer have Dave with us physically, his God given spirit lives on and it can truly be said, 'Well done, thou good and faithful servant'."
>
> —Don Sturtz

The Highway Dedication

Dave loved being a State Trooper and driving the roads of Ohio. Early in his career as a Patrolman, he loved to drive and stop and visit with people. Route 541 would have been one of those enjoyable roads.

Dave was born in Roscoe Village and Route 541 goes beside it. Route 541 goes through the main part of Coshocton beside Beech Avenue and Vine Street where he lived. It travels beside the new high school. Dave loved sports. His favorite sport was whatever was in season. The Route goes beside the factory where his mom worked and the church he attended.

As a child, Dave traveled all over the streets of Coshocton, probably crossing Route 541 all the time. He never knew a stranger in childhood or as an adult. Dave loved to talk with anybody and share a story.

Route 541, as you drive it, is rolling hills and valleys and winds through the countryside of Coshocton County. Dave loved the American Indian and as I have driven this route, I can hear Dave tell of Indian adventures through the area. I can hear his stories.

This Route is dedicated to Dave as The First Inspector General. He was privileged, as he said, to create the office from a piece of paper. On the paper was an Executive Order and during his tenure, the office became permanent. This highway is part of Dave's legacy not just as Inspector General but as a person. He would have been honored and humbled by this highway.

My hope is that as people drive it, they will remember Dave, google his name but more importantly, those of us who love him will be reminded that Dave's journey continues not just on this highway but in our hearts. He made a difference and continues to inspire and influence.

On this Sunday, October 22, 2017, we dedicate this highway in memory of David D. Sturtz and his legacy.

Made in the USA
Columbia, SC
18 August 2018